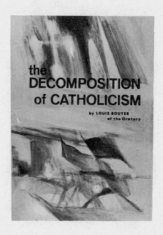

the
DECOMPOSITION
of CATHOLICISM

by LOUIS BOUYER
of the Oratory

THE DECOMPOSITION
OF CATHOLICISM   by Louis C. Bouyer, Or.

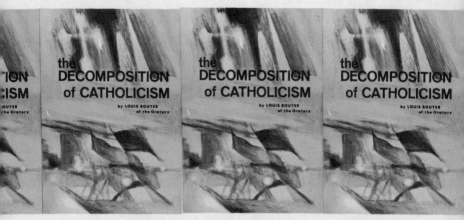

Translated, and with a foreword by CHARLES UNDERHILL QUINN

FRANCISCAN HERALD PRESS

THE DECOMPOSITION OF CATHOLICISM, first published in French under the title: *La Decomposition du Catholicisme*, by Aubier-Montaigne (Paris, 1968). Translated by Charles Underhill Quinn. Copyright 1969 by Franciscan Herald Press, 1434 W. 51st Street, Chicago, Illinois 60609. Library of Congress Catalog Card Number: 79-95292. Made in the United States of America.

NIHIL OBSTAT:
  Mark Hegener, O.F.M.
  Censor Deputatus

IMPRIMATUR:
  Rt. Rev. Msgr. Francis W. Byrne
  Vicar General, Archdiocese of Chicago

September 11, 1969

"The Nihil Obstat and the Imprimatur are official declarations that a book or pamphlet is free of doctrinal or moral error. No implication is contained therein that those who have granted the Nihil Obstat and Imprimatur agree with the contents, opinions, or statements expressed."

FOREWORD

Louis Bouyer needs no introduction to American readers, and to write a foreword for this short, but by no means insignificant work of a man whose work I have known and admired for many years seems both superfluous and arrogant. His books on the liturgy and patristic theology are unequalled classics in their fields, and only history will tell us the full extent of his influence on the preparation for the second Vatican Council, not only in liturgy and theology, but also in ecumenism. His acerbity may at times have offended those who are unable to see the twinkle in his eye and sense the sharp wit that cuts through the sham and hypocrisy of so many self-appointed experts.

Yet, because this book comes as much from the heart as from the mind, perhaps a few short words from the translator may be helpful for American readers.

The immediate audience of Father Bouyer's remarks was, quite naturally, French. As a Frenchman, and especially as a convert to the Roman Catholic Church, he is able to look at his own Church and the Church as a whole with a fresh, if not completely dispassionate, outlook. American readers, however, may not be fully aware of some of the historical background of the French Church of the nineteenth century, or the political-religious situation in present-day France. It is here that my few remarks, I hope, will be of service.

Father Bouyer's thesis relies heavily on the evolution of the Church in France since the Revolution. It is no secret that throughout the last century the Church had enormous difficulty in adjusting to and even admitting the fact that its position in society had entirely changed. France was no longer the "eldest daughter of the Church," in which the monarchy and the hierarchy worked hand and glove in a "Christian" State, but an a-religious if not always antireligious republic. The short-lived restoration of the monarchy after the fall of the first Empire only aggravated the situation, as did the second Empire. By the end of the Franco-Prussian war, and the reestablishment of a new republic, the rift between the hierarchy and the State was practically complete. Throughout the century partisans of a republic or monarchy became almost synonymous with "anti-clericals" and "clericals."

But all was not serene even within the Church itself. Attempts at reform, reparation, renewal, revindication (but not reconciliation) were made. The most significant of these was led by a priest called Félicien-Robert de Lamennais. At first, as Father Bouyer will tell us, he tried to link up Christianity with a theoretical monarchical absolutism, and then after his disillusionment and a change of heart, he left institutional Christianity and opted for a kind of new absolutism of the masses. His theories never really fully took hold, but the two currents he started, it is Father Bouyer's thesis, continue down to the present day. In France, they are called *intégrisme* (a type of conservatism that wants to retain every jot and tittle of Catholic practice "as it always was") and *progressime* (generally identified with progressive elements in the Church and the political left). Although these "parties" have a very definite French coloration, they have their counterparts throughout the whole Catholic world (as we are consistently reminded by *The New York Times!*). A particularly extreme form of *intégrisme* rallied to a peculiar ultra-monarchist and ultra-nationalist movement which found its expression in a review called *Action française*. Its founder, Charles Maurras, was a self-confessed atheist (converted on his deathbed) who maintained that the only salvation for France was to be in a return to strong hereditary monarchy, closely aligned with the Church, which was to be its strongest arm. *Action française* was condemned by the Vatican, and one of its chief protagonists, the Jesuit Cardinal Billot, retired under a cloud.

I sincerely hope that these few words will enable those readers, who may possibly be somewhat unfamiliar with some of the historical and political references made by the author, to appreciate the great value of his thesis and to reflect on its very serious implications not only for the whole Church but for the Church in America as well.

CHARLES UNDERHILL QUINN

ONE

The pontificate of John XXIII, and then the Council, seemed to have inaugurated an unhoped for (if not undreamt of!) renewal in the Catholic Church. It is true that there had been a gradual rediscovery of the Bible and the Church Fathers; there was also the liturgical movement, ecumenism, and (through a return to the sources of theology and catechetics) a rediscovery of the Church herself in her most authentic tradition, combined with a determined opening out to the scientific, cultural and social problems of the world. But until this moment all of these things had seemed to be the private preserve of a small elite, easily suspect in high places, and of little influence with the general public. Suddenly, or at least rapidly, the whole movement began to win over the body of the Church through its having been imposed on her leaders. Only a few years have gone by since then, but, we must admit, what has followed so far does not seem to have produced much of a response to one's expectation. Unless we are blind, we must even state bluntly that what we see looks less like the hoped-for regeneration of Catholicism than its accelerated decomposition.

A ranking French politician, who is Christian but does not belong to the Catholic Church, was speaking to some of his co-religionists on the consequences of the Council. He said, if I am to have faith in what one of his hearers

3

told me, that we ought now to expect the disappearance of Catholicism in a generation. This unimpassioned and lucid opinion of an observer, who undoubtedly has little sympathy for his subject, cannot be lightly dismissed.

Doubtless, long experience has shown that prophecies of this kind, often re-echoed in the past, are quite rash. In the last century, the historian Macaulay observed that Catholicism has survived so many and such grave crises that it was now no longer possible to imagine anything that would bring its definitive downfall. But it would be too easy for Catholics to be reassured by such words, and then fall back into that lethargic torpor to which, today as in the past, they are only too inclined. Without wishing to be dramatic, we must acknowledge that once again (and perhaps more than ever before) we have reached one of those turning points in history where, if Providence is willing once more to come to our aid, she will do so only by raising up among us men whose vision measures up to the circumstances and whose courage is equal to their insight.

What we need first of all is to clearly see into ourselves. In this domain it seems that in recent times we have merely exchanged a paralyzing form of self-satisfiedness for a still more pernicious euphoria. The "triumphalism" of yesterday, rightfully denounced, caused us to greet as a series of victories the most hastily remedied (if not merely camouflaged) reverses. We can laugh at the style, which has abruptly become obsolete, of our *Semaines religieuses.* But the new Catholic press has not been long in secreting a "neo-triumphalism" that is hardly more worthwhile and which may be worse. A French weekly which calls itself "Catholic" went so far recently as to inform us that the postconciliar renewal has not really penetrated the Spanish Church, using as a criterion the fact that the number of

priestly and religious vocations has not decreased very
much in that country! When we have reached Knock's
viewpoint, where persistent signs of health are interpreted
as symptoms of a particular gravity, the illness must be
quite advanced; only it is the physician's mind that is obviously the sickest!

That illustration might seem merely amusing, but it
demonstrates one of the most significant aspects of our
present crisis. I do not know whether, as we are told, the
Council has freed us from the tyranny of the Roman Curia,
but what is sure is that, willy-nilly, it has handed us over
(after having first surrendered itself) to the dictatorship
of the journalists, and particularly the most incompetent
and irresponsible among them.

It was undoubtedly very difficult to maintain the se-
cretness of the deliberations of such a large assembly. A
certain amount of publicity, furthermore, could be advan-
tageous, and not merely because public opinion, as Pius XII
recognized, has become a factor of modern society that no
one may overlook or ignore. A council, and especially in the
circumstances that this one was held, is of concern to the
whole Church. And, as we shall further elaborate, it would
be a very restricted view of the role of authority that
would suppose that the Council is of concern to the whole
body of the Church only in its decisions. In the Church
authority cannot be fruitfully exercised in a vacuum. If it
resigns from its role by merely passively recording the various opinions floating about among the faithful, it is equally impossible to fulfill it when it ignores these ideas. But
the *consensus fidelium* is something quite different from
a public opinion that is manipulated and even prefabricated
by a press which, even when it is not completely led off
the track by its pursuit of the sensational, remains hardly

or not at all capable of grasping the real import of the questions under consideration, or simply their true meaning.

And, it must be said, whatever respect we may have for our bishops and for the conscientiousness with which they wished to perform their task in the council, many of them were ill-prepared to exercise their role amid the blasts of such a clamorous publicity which was so often motivated by concerns that had very little in common with what they should have been. Under these circumstances we ought not be too surprised, especially during the last sessions of the Council, if many of the Fathers' interventions and reactions were much more "conditioned" (doubtless without their realizing it!) by a concern to please their new masters. Congressmen have long known that the death of the parliamentary system is not far off when they begin to speak, as they do, less to shed light on the question at hand than to obtain a *satisfecit* from their constituencies, and advocate an opinion formed for them by a snatch-and-grab press. As novices in the game, those bishops who allowed themselves to be more or less used by these old hands were certainly excusable. But we should realize that if in this Council (as in every preceding one) the internal intrigues and factions within the assembly were not its most edifying trait, this new type of external pressure (undoubtedly because it *was* new) showed itself to be no less detrimental than the muddle-headed intervention of the emperors and the different political powers in the past.

We should immediately add that the years that followed have abundantly shown that the bishops were surely not the only ones in the Church to lose their footing and sometimes their heads as a result of the head-turning appeal of a particular kind of journalism. We have since seen some of the seemingly most solid theologians give in

to the temptations of an interview with the naiveté of con-
ceited children, ready to say anything as long as the professional sophists of our time might confirm them in the eyes
of a supposedly passive public. One of the most thoughtful
and best-informed thinkers we have in Catholic tradition
made himself look ridiculous from the outset in a country
where he had never been before by roundly condemning the
local episcopate (all he knew about it was from the people
who had taken him under their wing on his arrival); afterwards he launched into a raving apology for homosexuality.
This gives us evidence of the weakness of the "great"
theologians when they step out of their cells to expose
themselves in front of television lights (sometimes more
dangerous perhaps for them than the fires of concupis-
cence).

If the press, and particularly the Catholic press, had
limited itself to furnishing exact information about the
Council, it could have done the most basic thing one could
ask for in contributing to its success. The press could have
played a more elevated role by contributing toward en-
lightening the conciliar Fathers themselves on the profound
aspirations, or still more simply the needs and problems of
the faithful and the modern world in general. More delicate,
but by no means impossible, would have been its task of
expressing the thoughtful reactions and even the most bit-
ing criticisms, if even partially well-founded, not only of the
"experts" (who were not all at the Council) but of men of
good will who were more or less qualified to know the questions treated.

Something of this certainly did take place, although
we must point out that the specifically Catholic press or the
Catholic newsmen in the secular press were not always
among those who deserved the accolade. Too often since

then those supposed experts, who were most willing to play at being journalists, seemed tiresomely inclined to adopt the worst irregularities of their new craft by seeking out the sensational and even the scandalous when they were not imposing their own disputable points of view with every means including slander and blackmail. After that, we need not complain too much if professional journalists did not do much better.

Since that time this phenomenon has only grown and become more complex. Most of the theologians who courted the "great" press contracted, with sometimes caricatural excess, these glaring vices so cheerfully that it makes us wonder about the roots of their attachment to the truth. When we see them today, in closed ranks, sending thunderous condemnations of pontifical encyclicals to the press before even having had time to read them, in order to attempt to get ahead of, and if possible surpass, the daring of the secular or non-Catholic commentators themselves, we can begin to appreciate the gravity of the evil.

We can evaluate it completely only when we become aware of the hardly believable credulity with which these "guides presumptive" of Catholic opinion are able to accept foolish fables and then guarantee them for the unsuspecting public. Indeed, we are no longer dealing with interpretations, which are always disputable, but with facts, and in many cases, with those facts that we can attain with a bit of honesty and perspicacity. One revealing test has been furnished by a book on the personality of Paul VI published under an Armenian-sounding pseudonym. Semi-official publicity was employed to pass it off as the work of a diplomat who knew his way about in Roman circles. The fraud was so artless (obviously fictitious conversations, which even had they taken place would never have been

known to people who were not present, a total ignorance of
the characters and the authentic relations of the chief persons involved, etc.) that an American newsman was able
to unmask it the moment the book appeared. He had no
trouble in establishing that the "diplomat" in question was
in fact a young defrocked Irish Jesuit who spent only
time enough in Rome to gather the most inane gossip.
Yet subsequently, this book was still translated into French
and warmly recommended by Catholic periodicals that were
thought to be serious-minded. Informed of their mistake,
the editors side-stepped any rectification. Here we have our
finger upon the breach of honor (conscious or unconscious)
on the part of contemporary Catholic intelligentsia. In the
name of the modern need for free information, people are
ready to be taken in by the legends that would have made
Gregory of Tours pale, without a shadow of the critical
spirit. Moreover, once they have contributed towards their
public accreditation, out of false shame they refuse their
minimum duty to the truth, in that they have helped real
scoundrels to do their dirty work, by their blundering
stupidity.

The role of the press, and especially of the Catholic
press, is evidently quite substantial in our present confusion, which began at the time of the Council and since then
has increased. This is why it is fitting at this point to begin
to analyze the situation. What we have said is sufficient to
show that it is not in the only too common defects of the
contemporary news media that the source of the evil is to
be found. It seems that here we simply have a case of what
may be seen in many other areas besides that of the press.
At other periods, without always succeeding in totally
Christianizing the merely human institutions of which they
had become a part, Catholic Christians on the whole suc-

ceeded in introducing to them a certain purification, and
even an undeniable nobility; whatever we might think of
the empire of Constantine and his successors, it was better
than the empires of Nero or Commodius. Without in any
way being a model, the medieval knight gave evidence of
virtues that his predecessor, the barbarian *Reiter,* certainly
did not possess. And despite his limitations, the Christian
humanist of the Renaissance was still far superior to those
of his fellows who did not share his views.

Today, is it merely by chance that the coming of Christians, and especially Catholics, into the contemporary
world arena only emphasizes the defects observed before
their arrival, if they do not add something of their own?
Is not what makes news for the press, or the media in
general, merely an equivalent of what may be seen in political parties or labor unions when Catholics make their appearance? From the extremists of the P.S.U., through
Action française and the M.R.P. (to say nothing of other
countries, such as the Center Party in Germany, the
Demochristians in Italy, the Franco regime, Catholic "rev-
olutionism" in South America), it is hard to avoid the impression that the "clerical party," whether of the Left, the
Right or the Center, almost universally goes along with the
unrealism, cliquishness, back-room politics, vapid wordiness
or the brutal violence that are common defects of modern
political parties, and that this same clerical party will soon
be pushing them to the point of the ludicrous and the
shocking. The same is true for the trade unionists. Once
colonized(in Europe at least)by Catholics, they seem hardly any longer to have a choice between the servility of the
"yellows" or the demagogy of the "reds."

Will modern Catholics be among those individuals
whom a congenital defect predisposes not only towards

catching every possible illness, but even towards mani-
festing a particularly virulent form of them? With them
grace seems to have stopped not only being *elevans* but
even *sanans*.

There are two not especially new virtues which are not
really exclusively Catholic even though they have suddenly
become active in contemporary Catholicism. They have
found an ideal culture medium in the workings of today's
press, and they are a mythology, substituted for the analysis of reality and a "sloganism" that has replaced doctrinal thought.

It is rather amusing to see the enthusiasm shown by
our "up to date" Catholics for Bultman and his "demy-
thologization," when we note the place they give to the fable
function, as a substitute for a proper awareness of what
is real.

This was evident from the very first sessions of the
Council and the accounts that were immediately popular-
ized. Their naive Manicheanism knew only black and white.
On the one hand there were the "bad guys," most of whom
were Italians with the rare exception of an Irishman or a
Spaniard. On the other side, the "good guys" were all non-
Italians with one or two exceptions. One party included the
Ottavianis, the Ruffinis, the Browns, the Heenans, and the
other the Frings', the Legers, the Suenens', and the Al-
frinks, merely to mention the *porporati*. The first group was
uniformly rascally, stupid and niggardly, while the second
was equally beyond reproach, bright and noble.

Such a created mythology fittingly bolstered the slo-
gans. On one side you had tradition (identified as the most
desperate obscurantism). While on the other party bespoke
complete newness in a noonday light. Authority was pic-
tured as against freedom (and *vice versa*). Doctrine was

opposed to pastoral considerations. Ecumenism quite comically played tricks on the unity, and even more the unicity, of the Church. The ghetto was contrasted to the open door to a world in confusion, etc.

Obviously, among the cardinals, as well as with other bishops, we must acknowledge that, whether we like it or not, there were more than one (even among the most renounced) who appeared to take no sides. Yet they were still classified at will when they asserted themselves too influentially in one or other category, even if they were suddenly recategorized in the other camp. As the great hope of the "whites" while he was still a cardinal, Giovanni Battista Montini had for a time been graced with the benefit of the doubt. However, once he became Paul VI he was reclassified among the "blacks." Actually, there would be many other men who were cross-classified and when we look at them more closely we find curiously that two times out of three it is a question of people best known for their fidelity to balanced and consistent positions. Inversely, since the Council, and even more in the Synod that followed, an analysis of the votes shows many times that the most supposed "whites" tended to close ranks with the "blacks," and even the most positive ones. It is still more striking if we observe what happened in the episcopal commissions set up in Rome for the implementation of the council. This fact is significant and we shall have to explain it at the proper time.

This reduction of the Council, and even more of what followed it, to a conflict between black sheep and spotless lambs has made us lose sight of the essential role of most of the true craftsmen of conciliar work, and at the same time has given ephemeral publicity to a few gadflies. What is more serious, however, is that it has sidetracked people from the real problems by regaling them with conflicts, which, even when they were real, were often superficial and furthermore their real meaning was almost never clearly untangled. Yet persons go while problems remain. And this is why the conciliar and post-conciliar mythology is most harmful when it directly coats this meaning.

In this area we must demystify especially those myths surrounding service and poverty ("The Servant Church of the Poor"), collegiality, ecumenism, the opening to the world and *aggiornamento*. What I mean is that these themes are indeed the most valuable acquisitions or rediscoveries of the Council, and I by no means wish to demean them. However, since the Council, we have seen them swell up and become deformed because of the condition I have just mentioned. And since then they have continued to be blown up today to the point of explosion. All we need is the prick of a pin and there would be nothing left but an empty balloon, still wet with saliva. Why be hesitant about doing it, except that he might appear to be attacking the realities themselves, which have merely been blown up out of proportion instead of being developed? Yet it has to be done if we want them to survive this period of edema which, if it lasts, will be fatal.

First of all, service. It is only too true that we have inherited from the baroque era not only a notion of the Church and her hierarchy dominated by the late medieval idea of power, but a peculiar life-style which gave much more evidence of the social upstart than the royal or seigneurial. Everybody cannot play the Sun King with impunity. But all the "princes" of the Church had adopted as a style imposed on them (even though they may have been very simple people) a kind of divine-right royalty and seemed to be able to breathe no other air than that of the Court.

The progressive swell of titles was revealing in itself: *reverendi* up to the seventeenth century became *reverendissimi*. This was not enough and when the cardinals replaced *illustrissimi*, with which they had been content until then, with *eminentissimi*, the bishops were quite ready. They did not quite dare "Highness" but they gave themselves the title Grace or Lordship before agreeing to Excellency. In France, the restoration of the monarchy after the Napoleonic era allowed them to be elevated to "Milord" (*Monsignore*), which the old regime had granted only to those six bishops who were peers of the realm.

The same is true with dress. At the same period they had begun to don the violet of the Roman prelacy. They had no purple and did not know that the violet was merely the pontifical livery, which in turn had been inherited from the signs of servitude worn during the empire by the public slaves (still today in Rome the cops, undertaker's assistants and scavengers have this right!) . . . But let us stop here. There would be too much to say. It is better merely to point out a few ridiculous things and let the ominous (which is certainly not absent!) drop.

The time was rife, more than rife, to recall first of all that the hierarchy is a "ministry," i.e. a "service," since with us it stands for Him who even as Lord and master wanted only to take the place and function of the "Servant" in becoming flesh. As Father Congar has so well established, it was not enough to say that the sacred functions were to be excercised in a spirit of service (which has always been said, or at least mouthed), but to rediscover that they *are* a service. If the reading of the Gospel, the Epistles of St. Paul and St. Peter is not enough, we have only to reread the letter from St. Gregory the Great to the patriarch of Constantinople.

And just as the Church leaders themselves, beginning
with the highest, could have no higher aim than to be "servants of the servants of God," it was important to acknowledge that the entire Church in the world is called upon to
serve mankind and not to dominate it (even for its supposed "good").

All that is well and good. Unfortunately, and it is here
that we fall short of the Gospel and into mythology, it
seems that modern Catholics are not capable, when they say
"servant," of thinking of anything but a domestic syco-
phant. This makes one wonder if their triumphalism of
yesterday was nothing else but a flunkey mentality, parad-
ing under a shabby gentility, trying to forget that it is
nothing more than the luxurious raiment of their aliena-
tion. The mentality seems not to have changed. Merely its
outer forms have become unfashionable.

To say that Church ministers, beginning with the leaders,
are servants has therefore come to mean that they no longer need take their responsibility as leaders and teachers
seriously, but rather follow the flock instead of leading the
way. The following tasty morsel has been attributed to the
colonel of the *Garde Nationale* at the time of its disband-
ment in 1848: "Since I am their leader, it is quite natural
that I follow them." Sometimes (should we not say often?)
we get the impression that today's bishops, and in their
wake all our doctors of the law, have made this their
motto. Priests and faithful can say whatever they want,
ask for whatever they want: *vox populi vox Dei.* Everything is blessed with a perfect indifference, but preferably
everything of which we should have been ashamed before
the Council. "What is truth?" Pilate said. Those responsible seem to have no other reflex answer than: "Whatever
you wish, my friends." The Kingdom of God belongs to the

violent who have taken possession of it. It would be said
that these words are now understood in the too facile sense
that the Kingdom of God is up for grabs. Newman was
eclipsed for twenty years for having been unfortunate
enough to have mentioned this historical truth. The Council of Nicaea was followed by a kind of suspension of authority for a whole generation. Vatican II will have been
followed by a kind of general resignation by the teaching
Church. How long? And who cay say?

The late Father Laberthonnière remarked with that abil-
ity to simplify that was both his strong and weak point:
"Constantine made an empire out of the Church, St. Thomas
made her a system and St. Ignatius a constabulary." He
would have some excuse today to say that the Council had
made her into a place of total enjoyment and no responsibility like Thélème Abbey.

But this is not the worst. That is to be found in what has
been made of the idea that the Church is at the service of
the world. The Church — we are told — no longer has to
convert the world, but to become converted to it. She no
longer has anything to teach it, and must only listen to it.
But what about the Gospel of salvation? Is that not completely responsible for the world? Does its essential service
not constitute bringing the Gospel to the world? Ah, but
wait! We have changed all that. As the title of a typically
post-conciliar book tells us, it is the "salvation in the Gospel" that has become our Gospel. Yet, since we are here in
a kind of poker game where one person's bluff merely spurs
on the rest to the same end, this formula is already out of
date. As I was told recently by one of our new theologians,
the very idea of salvation is an insult to the world as God's
creation. Man today cannot accept it! Let's not talk about
it any more! But can that be enough? Does not the man of

today think that it is an even more unbearable insult to suppose or insinuate that he is a creature of God? God is dead, didn't you know? If you did not, it is because you don't read the "in" Catholic publications! If He is dead, He should be all the less qualified to be a creator! . . .

In other words, to serve the world no longer means anything but pampering it and giving it adulation, just as we did in the past to the parish priest and the diocesan bishop, and just as we hyperadulated the pope on St. Peter's chair. Is that not natural if serving the Church itself is not first of all serving it the truth of the Gospel? . . . If as a result of a sudden appetite for fatherhood our high priests as well as our priests of second or twenty-fifth rank are so ashamed of their inveterate paternalism that they really do not want to be fathers any more, but sugar grand-daddies who have resigned from their rearing function, being capable solely of knowing how to spoil their offspring?

Poverty is on all fours with service. Consequently, we must expect one to be as good as the other.

It would not be an exaggeration, perhaps, to say that the evolution whereby the Old Testament prepared for the New is nowhere more striking than in the growing emergence of the theme of poverty. At the beginning the riches of the earth seem to be pure divine blessings (as we can see from the patriarchial blessings at the end of Genesis). Isaiah, who himself was a man of means, still strikes the first strident note in exclaiming: "Woe to the rich!" With Jeremiah and the last psalms it is the poor man, whose sole riches are his faith, who becomes the blessed one of God. At the first words of the Sermon on the Mount Jesus proclaimed: "Blessed are the poor! . . ." This is the underlying theme in the whole of Luke's Gospel. And St. Paul sums up Christ's work for us by saying that though he was rich he made himself poor for us. Here too there is much to be desired in Holy Church after twenty centuries! If the Jews have the reputation of being moneyed, rightly or wrongly, the clergyman's reputation is no less well established. I myself once heard Cocteau quote a sublime phrase that he had got from Lehmann, the director of the *Opéra*: "To think that in the beginning the Jews had a business venture like the Catholic Church and they let it get out of their hands! . . ."

Poverty is so important in Christianity that "religious," as they are called, have always had the acknowledged task of giving evidence of it by exemplary radicalism. But it is stating a truism to recall that their life-style in most cases, today and for a long time past, is in fact much less poor than that of the great majority of the so-called "secular" clergy, and reflects rather the average level of a free and easy middle class. In a talk on religious poverty I once had the misfortune to underline this discrepancy of fact between it and evangelical poverty. I have not forgotten the very edifying responses made to me. One of the most celebrated Catholic moralists of the time, a member of the Society of Jesus (where, especially in France, poverty is much stricter than in other religious institutes), retorted that my views were implicitly condemned by canon law. This, said he, makes religious poverty consist in the renunciation of individual property, and not of the use of collective possessions, whatever they may be. A scholarly Dominican theologian immediately aligned himself with him and did him one better (the words fit the situation). St. Thomas Aquinas, he wished to explain to me, established that by itself the vow of poverty honors God much more and much better than any practice in the concrete of material poverty . . .

If the Church's poverty experts have arrived at this point, it is not too surprising that some of our non-religious are still less worried by the problem. The taste for gaudy and useless buildings (which, like Lisieux or Nazareth, are generally abominations), the life-style of high-ranking clergy, the charge-scale for acts of worship and especially for dispensations are but trifles when compared with more profound and hidden evils. What should be said about the principle, admitted by the moralists, that simony (the selling of spiritual realities, or more generally any temporal benefice connected with their being dispensed) does not exist when we are dealing with a practice authorized by law (hence, for example, certain scandalous traficking with mass stipends, which is all the more scandalous precisely because this happens not only with the connivance of the highest authorities but many times at their instigation)? And more, what should we say about the innumerable "works" encouraged to solicit the faithful, when everyone knows that they are more profitable for their organizers than for the salvation of souls — to say nothing about the glory of God? Above all, what is to be said about the general waste of monies collected, the bulk of which was to have gone to the maintainance of the apostolic clergy, although everyone also knows, in France particularly, what portion they receive for their living, with the exception of a few "plush pastors" whom chanceries treat like farmers-general?

This is to say, and there will be many other things to say about it, that a return to the Gospel is pre-eminently necessary here. And we must add that it is all the more necessary since we are in an age where the development of material civilization has brought to an extreme the difference in living between the rich and poor peoples, so that the spectacle, for example, of missionaries living with every American comfort (including air-conditioning) in the midst of the deprivation of the Asian or African populations they were supposed to be evangelizing, became a much more convincing counter-evangelization than their sermons. Let us not forget in the West itself, and especially in its most underprivileged areas like Latin America, the shocking collusion of the clergy, beginning with the hierarchy, with the profiteers of a social system that is both iniquitous and a misfit.

Most excellent papers were heard at the Council on this subject. Yet we may be permitted to regret that certain of the most eloquent were given by well-known clergy-businessmen and we do not know whether they have modified their behavior since. Take the example of a bishop of Spanish language but not nationality who runs an under-the-counter publishing house. It puts out only translations, because the country in which he lives has not ratified the international conventions, thus dispensing him from paying any author's royalties and even any recompense to the copyright-holding publishers. I do not know how such operations are called in the Church (it has already been seen that I am not a professional moralist), but I know that in the world they are called rackets. But finally, as St. Paul says, even when the Gospel is not preached with a pure intent, we must still rejoice that it is being preached at all!

What we might legitimately ask, however, is that a realistic application follow upon doctrine. Here, once again, we find ourselves rather wide of the mark. We must admit that since the Council even preachers more upright than the one to whom I have just alluded have not seemed very clear on an essential point: must the Church *become* poor or merely *appear* so?

From the moment that this theme of poverty made its entrance into the aula of the Council, the press warned us that a group of bishops had resolved to devote themselves especially to its triumph or its exploitation (I apologize for not finding better terms). They called themselves, or allowed themselves to be called "the Church of the catacombs" for after calling the reporters they met discreetly in subterranean and funereal places where, as we have long known, the persecuted Church never actually assembled, whatever the romantics may have thought. People waited aflutter for the momentous decisions to which they would commit themselves, in order to involve a mass of less conspicuously ascetical prelates. We learned with wonder that they had decided to drive their own motor cars (which would dispense with the salary but also the livelihood of their drivers), no longer to have a bank account in their own names, but in the name of their "works" (although they apparently retained the signatory right), and above all to use only croziers and crosses made of wood (a glance in the catalogues is enough to show that today these objects of equal workmanship are more expensive in wood than in metal) . . . In other words, with these pioneers the concern for appearances easily won out over a concern for essentials. Yet it is precisely here and not elsewhere that the problem lies. As one of these religious told me, there are still men who are not juridically poor, but really poor: "Why so much concern about seeming poor? If one really is, people will see it quite by themselves!" Yes, but we may rightly wonder to what extent we want to be poor, and to what extent we are looking for an illusion to seem poor and thus escape the actual need to become so.

For, and this is the prime difficulty, once we are so very concerned about opening out to the world, accepting the

world and consecrating it as it is (although today it is fact
and wishes only to be a society of production and consump-
tion) how can we really conceive of selling all we have and
giving to the poor, and then following Christ? For all we
can do, we cannot do everything at once!

Thus, to my knowledge up till now this great crusade
for the poor Church has accomplished little else but the
impoverishment of worship. A certain bishop, whose cathe-
dral possesses a treasury of wonderful old vestments, since
his return from the Council now officiates, surrounded by
his brocade-vested chapter, in a sack cloth . . . It is true
that afterwards he returns home in a Citroën, while the
most comfortable of his canons may not even have a tiny
2 CV.

I must confess, and I am not alone in this, that I find
these candle-stub economies particularly degrading. It is
the poverty of Judas and not of Christ. Worship is a
thing that belongs both to God and to the whole people of
God. It is a celebration in which everyone from the poorest
to the richest is at home in the house of the Father and is
called to rejoice in his presence. Luxury and tawdry showi-
ness are surely out of place, but real and even costly beauty
could not find a better place in this world. We are told that
great churches which are also works of art will no
longer be built because they are an offense to the indigent.
Are they? The Anglicans of the last century who well before us made the greatest effort to establish contact with
the most deprived urban proletariat, thought quite the contrary that it was honoring the poor to come to them not
only with bread and soup tickets or even the most effective
social works, but also to give them churches no less beautiful and a more splendid liturgy than those of the upper-
class neighborhoods. And to do this they did not hesitate

to fleece these more affluent parishioners. Out of this came
churches like St. Peter's, London Dock, which were soon
filled with a people of God that was not exactly aristo-
cratic. These were to be the beginning both of the spread
of Anglicanism into areas it had never reached and of a
popular liturgical movement next to which our own appears
quite paltry.

Moreover, the idea that a hodge-podge worship will necessarily cost less than a splendid one is childish. Even if
quality liturgical art is relatively costly (no more and often
much less than the tawdriest), what would be stopping the
building of churches or altars worthy of the name, or ceas-
ing to make priestly vestments that are not niggardly or
hideous, do for the poor? It would suddenly enrich all those
petty tradesmen who already extract only too much money
from the clergy by soliciting them to accept their lines of
supposedly inexpensive trash, but it would pauperize a lot
of craftsmen or workers who most deserve our concern.
And does not the Church need artists as well as scholars
to announce the Gospel in the culture of each age? Yet today her clergy scorn artist and scholar alike, however incapable they may be at telling them apart from barbers or
authors of cross-word puzzles!

Beneath these stingy economies there remains the old
confusion between charity and "do-gooding," a confusion
that has never been more deceptive than in our own day. It
is even less true today than ever that helping the poor
means melting down one's gold, supposing one has any, in
order to give them bread. But both before and after the
Council an organization of mendicancy on a world scale
remains the best that Catholics seem to have come up with
for the alleviation of the world's hunger. The horrible tragedy of Biafra ought to have opened their eyes since tons of

food and medicine gleaned from the four corners of the
earth went to rot on the doorstep of the needy because of
a lack of elementary good will on the part of the local people. Yet this is only a particularly obvious example of a
quasi-universal situation. What is the use of sending full
cargos of wheat to India at great cost to alleviate an epi-
demic famine? Either the dockers will be too lackadaisical
to unload it before it goes bad, or else it will be stored in
wretched hangars to be devoured by monkeys or rats, or
else it will be re-sent by corrupt functionaries to richer
countries for the price of gold. In any case, what would
they do with it? Since the departure of the English there
are no railways or roads in India that would permit the dis-
tribution of this wheat—and, what is more, Indians do not
eat bread but rice! The only effective aid to the under-
developed countries that Christians can provide is to help
develop themselves. But here we should need a bit more
imagination than was needed to organize the *Secours Cath-
olique International*—a perfectly honorable institution, as is
proved by the fact that its budget devotes barely half of
its resources to the upkeep of its collaborators (something
one could not say of the charitable organizations of the UN,
nor of our French social security system!).

However, when in this area post-conciliar Catholics want
to give evidence of this imagination (which to them seems
so sparsely distributed), they have but one word on their
lips. Naturally it is one more myth, one that they are taking up with at the very moment when to practically everyone else it seems singularly old hat. This myth, of course,
is "revolution"! Which one, you might ask? Moscow's?
The recent events in Prague are still too fresh in our minds
for us not to impugn that; we need time to forget, although
not too much time (remember Budapest!) While we are

waiting, it might be Mao with his "cultural revolution" un-
leashing on the traditional intellectuals the furor of the
people, after the collapse of the people's communes and
the resulting period of want. Or how about Fidel Castro?
He may not as yet have succeeded in making people pine
for the sinister Batista (human capacities do have their lim-
its), but he has certainly done still more to aggravate the
deplorable economic system he inherited, to the point that
if the Russians stopped feeding Cuba for a week, not only
would the regime collapse but everyone would die of hunger.

Our Catholic friends of the poor have big hearts and are
ready indifferently to uphold all these ultimate exploiters
of human misery, but they obviously prefer the P.S.U. (a
non-Communist French Socialist party of the far left).
There, one can be most generous in words, and with the
exception of a few blessings of barricades or Molotov cock-
tails made by students (generally from upper class back-
grounds), one does not seem to have any chance of having
to act in the near future . . .

But I shall be speaking again about the politics of Catholics and (I assure you!) from all quarters, Right, Left
and even the Center, so that everybody will be happy or at
least have his own dressing down. For the moment let us
continue our little mythological study.

When John XXIII had just been elected and came out of
the Sistine Chapel, he said to those about him: "I want
my pontificate to restore collegiality in the Church."
This could indeed have been the most significant achieve-
ment of the Council instead of merely canonizing the
principle. Not only as men to succeed him, but from the
beginning of his earthly ministry, Jesus surrounded himself with twelve disciples whom he involved in all of his
concerns. After the Passion, Resurrection and Ascension,

it seems obvious that Peter was to be the spokesman for this community and also its responsible leader. Nevertheless, he always acted in conjunction with his colleagues, and when a grave problem arose, even though it may have been settled in his own mind (as in the story of the centurion Cornelius and the first evangelization of the pagans) he put it up or permitted it to be put up for discussion among the Twelve. This was what is somewhat pompously (but very rightly, if we go to the heart of the matter) called the "Council of Jerusalem," described in the Acts of the Apostles. But we must go further. We see in the New Testament that the apostles themselves also were not interested merely in providing successors. They first wanted collaborators whom they associated as closely as possible with their work and their decisions. And there is still a further point. If the Church was not thought to have been actually founded until Pentecost, it is doubtless because the Holy Spirit descended upon it at this moment, but it is also because it was at that time that the first apostolic preaching gathered the first believers around the witnesses of the Resurrection. And we should note that the Spirit did not descend on the preachers only, but conjointly upon the believers. "The laity? What is that?" groused a bishop to Newman. He was content to answer: "Well! Without them the Church would look rather foolish!"

In two words, the Church is a people, the People of God in which there are leaders responsible for it. But also, on every level between the leaders and the other members, there is a community of life with common concerns because there is a common faith. Surpassing and animating all this, there is a fellowship in the one Spirit, who dispenses his gifts to all, and to each his own gift. But all the gifts, the highest as well as the lowliest, are for the good of all, and necessary for all. And the greatest gift, served by all the others, is charity. Once again that does not mean any abdication on the part of the responsible leaders. Quite the contrary, after having said the substance of what precedes to the Corinthians, St. Paul was not ashamed to tell them their four truths, but also to inculcate in them what they were to believe and do, whether it pleased them or not, because this was his function and he had received it from Christ. But that means certainly that the Church could not be divided into two: a teaching Church superimposed upon a taught Church, without any exchange between the two, nor still less an active Church which alone would have the capacity for stimulating a simply passive Church, and would be the only judge as to whether this should happen or not.

There is no room for doubt that once again at the eve of the Council we were rather far away from a frank acknowledgment of the doctrine. And if, as is always the case, once we are no longer content with perishing in a straitjacket of dead formulas, the life of the Church compensated to some extent for the narrowness of current theology, and still more the routinism of canon law, it was considerably fettered. We had practically reached a notion of the Church that was not so much monarchical as it was pyramidal, the worst thing being that the pyramid was supposed to stand on its head. On the level of the episcopate, when we read the manuals, and observe the practice of the Curia, we could easily be persuaded that the pope was everything and the bishops nothing. Similarly on the diocesan level, the bishop was everything and the priests nothing. On the parish level, the pastor was everything and the parishioners nothing. In sum, on all levels, each was a Janus, who wore a zero on one forehead and infinity on the other. Only the pope had the right to infinity alone, and only the *vulgum pecus* to zero . . . In fact, let us repeat, things were quite far from turning out this way, except in the manuals.

Pius XII may be described as the last (up to now) of the autocratic popes. But when we reread his most famous encyclicals (*Mystici corporis*, on the Church; *Mediator Dei*, on the liturgy; or *Divino afflante Spiritu*, on Holy Scripture), we must acknowledge that they regularized and therefore tried to organize three movements of thought and life; and it would be difficult to hold that they were born in Rome or that they spread out of Rome.

Similarly, after three months of the Council and the forced absence of the bishops, one not especially cynical vicar general told me: "It is three months now that we have practically no longer had an archbishop, and no one has noticed it yet . . .", and still the particular archbishop was not a nonentity. And whatever may be the unquestionable and furthermore unquestioned merits of modern Catholic Action, we must acknowledge that the laity did not wait for it before they took the initiative — which was not always to the taste of their immediate shepherds. And like many greater than they, in the long run they generally resigned themselves to chaperoning them, since at least that experience made them give up the hope of neutralizing them. But who was it that said that things that go without saying, generally go much better when said? If the Council had limited itself to this, it would already have done quite enough. However, it did do more and better.

On the level of the episcopate, it was concerned with defining the relationship between collegiality and the exercise of authority proper to the Sovereign Pontiff, with a detailedness that has sometimes appeared tiresome, but

which was also necessary in order to establish that episcopal collegiality was in no way opposed or opposable to
pontifical infallibility as defined at the first Vatican Council, and that this infallibility itself, far from doing away
with the reality of collegiality, is inseparable from it. As for
the role of the laity, it proclaimed the similar correlation
that must be recognized between the priesthood of the
faithful and the ministeral priesthood. On the other hand,
we have not yet arrived at the point of defining quite as
concretely their way of interacting. We ought not to be surprised at this, perhaps, for even with the greatest specialists like Fr. Congar the theology of the laity suffers
from a duality of viewpoints that have hardly found a
synthesis. To say on the one hand that the laity possesses
an authentic participation in the priesthood, an inherent
consecration and an effective capacity for consecrating
the world to God by what they do, and to maintain on the
other hand that their particular vocation is in a "consecration of the secular realities, even as secular" remains little
satisfying. These statements contain an ambiguity which
might allow us to suspect that two heterogeneous notions
of the laity survive side by side and that we shall sooner
or later have to choose between them.

But, we must admit, one of the weakest points of the
conciliar declarations is the little that they contain about
the priests of second rank, and especially that it *is* so little
in view of the fact that in the contemporary Church
particularly the whole of concrete pastoral work rests with
them. In the past, the episcopate had been transformed
into a kind of seigneurial caste, but since the Napoleonic
church it has come to concentrate on almost purely
administrative tasks which seem to have been rather the
job of deacons in the early church. They also wanted to

restore the diaconate but do not know quite what exactly they want to do with it.

Whatever these lacunae may be, there was in the conciliar texts at least, the principle, and once again more than the principle, of a restoration of the normal life of the Church as that of a body with members endowed with differing but harmonized functions. Alas! Nowhere perhaps does the distance seem as wide between these rediscoveries and the wretched residue to which we see them reduced in practice in so short a time. The rediscovery of collegiality implies two intimately connected things. One is the equivalent of what modern Russian Orthodox theology, following Khomyakov, has so well developed with the notion of *sobornost*, defined as "unanimity in love." And further, the idea which Möhler (whom Khomyakov himself called "the great Möhler") had so felicitously expressed: that the "service" of the "ministers" on all levels, pope, bishop, or priest, is basically the service of this unity in love which is but one with the unity in truth, since Christian truth is the truth of supernatural love. But in fact, never do we seem to have been further from either. Today "collegiality" seems merely a synonym for anarchy and, incredibly, for individualism.

After the Protestant Reformation one of our good writers said: "every Protestant was a pope, Bible in hand." On the whole, Catholics today do not bother with the Bible any more than they did yesterday. But since the pope took off his tiara at the Council, a vast number of people seem to believe that it descended upon their own heads. Each one seems to have discovered for himself a vocation as a Doctor of the Church. They do not only perorate to everyone indiscriminately and on every subject, but pretend to dictate the law with an authority inversely proportioned to their competence. And even those who have studied slightly what they are speaking about, too frequently are not satisfied with systematically ignoring authority's directives (to the extent that they are still given); they no less deliberately ignore every opinion that is not their own, and expect nothing else from this authority but the total, exclusive and immediate consecration of their own views, practices, and crotchets . . .

It was not so long ago that Catholics looked down their noses at the pulverization of Protestantism into rival and antagonistic sects or schools. To arrive in a twinkling of an eye at a still worse situation, all Catholics needed was the loosening of their own iron corset in which they had been imprisoned since the Reformation and to which the suppression of modernism had given the last turn of the screw. No one any more believes or practices except what he fancies. But the last parish assistant or the young chaplain of Catholic Action, just like the most ill-informed journalist, solves everything with infallible certitude. He is scandalized when the pope (let us not speak about other bishops!) permits himself an idea other than his, and he judges it unbearable that other priests or faithful are able to think in a way different from his. Certainly each wants freedom, but for himself, and it is primarily the freedom not to take other's opinions into account.

The most paradoxical point of the situation is this: at the moment we have lost all sense of authority! We are witnessing a kind of neo-clericalism, both lay and clerical, come alive again. It is more limited, more intolerant and more fussy than anything we had ever known before.

A typical example is that of liturgical Latin. Explicitly, the Council upheld the principle of keeping this traditional language in the Western liturgy, although it opened the

door to the broadest exceptions whenever pastoral needs
would require a more or less extensive use of the vernacu-
lar. Yet the mass of the clergy who until then could not
have even conceived that the people's language would receive a place, except in the proclamation of the Word of
God, immediately jumped from one extreme to the other
and no longer wanted a word of Latin to be heard in the
church. "It is now the laity's time to speak," it seems, but
on this point as on all others, only the condition that they
keep docilely repeating what they are told. If they protest
and want, for example, to retain at least the familiar
chants of the ordinary Mass in Latin, they are told that
their protest is worthless. They are not "trained." There
is no reason to take account of what they say! (Which is
all the more curious since they are asking precisely for
what the Council recommended.) But the Council has a
broad back. Three-quarters of the time its name is brought
up, people are not appealing to its decisions or exhortations
but to an individual episcopal statement, in no way ratified
by the assembly (when they are not bringing up what some
theologian or some two-bit writer without mandate wanted
to see the Council approve, and even a supposed "development" of the Council, even when this development in question contradicts it word for word.

What is true about Latin is true also about the whole
liturgy, and it was all the more serious once the Council
proclaimed its centrality in the life and the entire activity
of the Church. It was once emphasized that the traditional
Churches, with the Catholic Church in the forefront, by
their objective liturgy, taken out of abusive clerical ma-
nipulation, would safeguard the spiritual freedom of the
laity, when faced with the easily invasive and oppressive
subjectivity of our clergy. But of this nothing remains.

Contemporary Catholics now have the right only to have the religion of their pastor, with all its idiosyncracies, its limitations, its mannerisms and its futilities.

The Princess of the Palatinate once described German Protestantism to Louis XIV with this formula: "In our country, everyone makes up his own little religion." Every priest, or almost every priest, is at this point today. All the faithful have to say is *Amen*. They are still blessed when the pastor's or the assistant's religion does not change every Sunday, at the whim of his reading, the foolery he has seen others at, or at his own pure fancy.

The present situation in Catholic worship has merely gone the same road as the least traditional and most undisciplined aspect of Protestantism. But there, at least there is a certain respect for the divine word among the ministers and a certain familiarity with it on the part of the laity, which assures them of finding in their most deficient services some compensation for clerical imperialism. Among Catholics, both clergy and faithful, despite the still unsuccessful sporadic efforts to break through an old crust of indifference and even mute hostility, the Bible remains a closed book, and the translations, as many as there are, have still not changed the situation very much. The quick reading of two meager fragments from an epistle and gospel at mass remains a formality. Even when the sermon following is called a "homily" today, it generally owes very little of its content to the readings (supposing it has a content and is not merely a litany of catch-phrases, an appeal for funds, a commentary on the announcements, or some politico-clerical diatribe). By this, the hamstrung laity are at the mercy of the high-handedness of the clergy. They can no longer even expect the Church's prayer from them, but only a mish-mash of hollow propaganda. They look upon themselves as summoned to bring their enthusiastic contribution to the liturgy, when they bellow insipid mouthings as if they were "acclamations."

But this situation is not enough for the egoism of many clerics. Not happy with trafficking with the biblical or liturgical texts at whim (often tendentious translations have already tried to file them down to the mode of the day) they want returned to them the freedom to improvise prayers. A liturgical magazine, once in the vanguard of the liturgical movement, was introducing the new eucharistic prayers to its readers, and concluded with a dissertation in which its author (a bishop!) began by warning us that he had not even taken the trouble to acquaint himself with the new texts sanctioned by authority and taken from the Bible and the most authentic tradition. (Why should he?) Whereupon he declared plainly that the only tolerable eucharist today is one that would liberally draw its themes from technological progress, secular mankind arrived at adulthood, etc. In other words, the self-glorification of man in place of the praise of divine grace, the prayer of the Pharisee instead of the Church's eucharist!

It is true that the clergy do not have a monopoly in the brainwashing of the contemporary Church. Those lay· "militants" who, overnight, have turned into so many "neo-clergymen," have nothing to be envious about. There are numberless faithful who are not in a flurry, belong to no "movement" but who are trying, and at times heroically, to put the Gospel into their whole lives and especially to apply the traditional teaching of the Church to their moral lives. Perhaps the most remarkable characteristic of *Humanae Vitae*, if not the most noticeable, is to have singled them out as the ones to whom the pastors owe the most concern, and to have brought them a source of comfort they had not expected. Hence the fury of a certain professional "laity" that arrogates to itself the exclusive right to speak for other lay people. They are boiling at the fact that the authority believed those laymen, who are not much talked about, but who act with fidelity, are perhaps more representative of the Church, and have in any case a right to so much esteem . . . There is no need to further multiply our examples. Whoever can shed light on the following points will understand the one we have just made, and this is crucial.

Ecumenism. Now that is truly the great discovery of contemporary Catholicism! God knows that yesterday's ecumenism was hermetically sealed. Not too long ago, one of the most influential prelates under Pius XII greeted me at Rome by saying: "Remember that in Rome we don't like Protestants. We prefer atheists by far. And we especially don't want them to become converts because we are too afraid of the spirit they might bring into the Church . . ." And God knows that that was true only in Rome! Today, on the contrary, as an Anglican prelate said, what is more worrisome is the number and rapidity of the Catholic conversions to ecumenism. We may all begin to be suspicious about how so many people could change so quickly and so completely. And actually, when we look closer, it is least doubtful that many, and even the most exuberant, have understood what it is all about. Whoever speaks of ecumenism says nothing unless he is talking about Christian unity. But we are quite obligated to point out that the ecumenism of most Catholics of today shows no genuine interest in the substantive, and that one wonders if they have any more interest in the adjective. Lamennais said that George Sand was interested in socialism only for the odor of the lupanar she thought she smelled. Today's

Catholics similarly, seem to be overflowing with a sudden affection for Protestants, Anglicans and Orthodox (as well as for the Jews, the Turks and the Pagans), but not because they are awakening and at last responding to a felt need, to the increasingly more anxious desire of other Christians for the unity of the one Church, which, furthermore, would be the Church willed by Christ. On the contrary. It is what is most jumbled, inorganic and amorphous about the rest of Christianity that they have suddenly and gleefully discovered. But even that does not satisfy them and they want to flirt with every form of belief and especially non-belief. In other words, as one of the best contemporary ecumenists, a Protestant, observed with ironic sadness: "The greatest danger for ecumenism is that Catholics grow into enthusiasts for everything we have recognized as harmful, and abandon everything whose importance we have rediscovered." It is not the desire for unity among contemporary Protestants, particularly, that allures Catholics, and it is even much less the feeling that they as Catholics would have a responsibility towards their brothers as essential factors of this unity. It is much more their weariness of unity, their incapacity to understand its worth, their perverse curiosity, and their adulterated taste for schism and heresy — all of this at the very moment when other Christians, who are only too familiar with these attitudes, have finally begun in earnest to try and get rid of them!

Yet this is not what is most disheartening. That is the total ineptitude of the mass of "ecumenical" Catholics to perceive and respect what is most specific about ecumenism. They seem little able to understand that this is not solely a movement towards unity, and they have not yet found out, and stubbornly refuse to accept the fact, that it is a

Christian movement: the search for unity among *Christians*, for Christian unity. The program of most of the Catholic makeshift ecumenists seems to come down to the formula: "The more fools we are, the more we laugh!" Intercommunion with the Orthodox, the Anglicans, the Lutherans, the Reformed, etc. is not enough for them. Along with the Jews and the Muslims, they have to have it on a basis of perfect equality with the Buddhists, the Hindus, the Shintoists, the animists, and also with the Marxists, the existentialists, the structuralists, the Freudians, the atheists, the freethinkers and Free Masons of every complexion, and even the pederasts. But might we ask how one can have intercommunion with people who have no communion, who do not want to have any, and do not even know what it is? If you ask questions of this kind, it means you still have a preconciliar mentality!

The truth is that since the Council it is not simply Catholic truth that has become an empty word for an indefinite number of Catholics, but Christian truth itself: the truth of Christ. Whether others believe it or not makes no difference, or the difference has no importance.

And this brings us straight to the opening out on the world, which all of the "up-to-the-minute" Catholics have never distinguished from ecumenism itself.

It scarcely needs to be demonstrated that post-Tridentine Catholicism had need of such an opening out, and even, to use an even stronger word, a genuine conversion to the world (in the etymological sense of a turning towards it, seeing it, understanding it and striving to love it as it is). Merely read the handbooks of philosophy that only yesterday occupied the cleric's complete attention during his first years of study in seminary, and you will be sufficiently edified. Descartes, Leibniz, Kant, Hegel, Bergson,

etc. were presented as so many mischievous twerps, who
could be done away with by one syllogism or sorites. Marx
was a man with the knife between his teeth. Freud . . . a
dirty old man. Blondel or Le Roy . . . modernists of a quite
special perversity, since they persisted in remaining Catholics while doubting that the only adequate philosophical
reasoning had to be in the *barbara* or *baralipton* forms!
Not so long ago at an international congress on apologetics
I saw with my own eyes and heard with my own ears a professor of a pontifical university demonstrate that men like
Gabriel Marcel who claimed to have come to the faith
through existentialism could be nothing but hypocrites. (I
recall also, thank God, the roars of fury with which Etienne
Gilson greeted this nonsense. They let him speak because no
one in that learned assembly knew his St. Thomas as well
as he, but from this to the point of bowing to his reasoning
was too much of a step!)

Need we recall the comic and lamentable story of poor
Charles du Bos? He was tortured morally for years in the
chapel of clerics (and laymen!) into which he had fallen
(naively taking it for the great choir of the Catholic
Church) because St. Augustine had brought him back to
the faith, and because it seemed that since the encyclical
Pascendi St. Augustine himself smacked of heresy!

Let us go on to science. It was hardly long ago that one
of the teachers of neo-Thomism (and far from the most
amateurish) demonstrated, syllogistically of course, that
evolution was a false problem since the "more" cannot come
from the "lesser." Still closer to our own time, when Fr.
Fessard was attempting to explain that a congenital weakness of Thomism was that it made no place for history, two
"experts" hastened simultaneously to take him to task.
One, however, demonstrated that this was precisely its su-

periority, while the other showed that it had the most superior view of history because its view was completely *a priori.*

What about arts and letters? If we accept Stendhal's
semi-historical definition that romantic art is any art that
seeks to give us pleasure, and classical art any art that
might have given pleasure to our grand-parents. Catholic
classicism can serve as a paradigm. The fact the Claudel's
neo-baroque style and the interminable medieval mastica-
tion and borborygmic style of Péguy could have seemed
disturbingly brazen to the most daring Catholics of yesterday, says quite a bit. And we need not look twice at the
church buildings "from the Cardinal's building-yard"
(leaving aside the pseudo-Monegasque constructions with
which at the same period Pius XI embellished the Vatican)
to be dispensed from explaining what art, and especially
"sacred" (?) art meant for them.

To give them their due, their middle-class tastes made
them more accessible to technological advances, although
seminaries and many institutions made a last stand against
modern hydrotherapy and sanitation.

In politics, it was not, as is sometimes thought, any romantic taste for lost causes, but simply laziness of imagination that made them the last defenders of the old order
when democracy was triumphing, identified them with
parliamentary democracy at the moment it was falling into
its dotage, and would make them fly to the aid of Marxism,
although its probably irremediable decline would be visible
to everyone, except them.

In a word, whether they turned to the world to bless it
or curse it, to rail at it or save it, Catholics, like that am-
putee who could not get it into his head that he had lost
his leg at Waterloo, were always in a world that no longer
existed and could snigger foolishly at the only world that

was contemporary to them. More precisely, for their own strictly personal use they made their own little world, with its philosophy that resembled a puzzle, its amusing and inoffensive science, no history, a literature of pious dressmaker's assistants and an art of practicing wig-makers, decrepit comfort facilities, and, to be more safe, laughable political parties and labor unions (their effectiveness was total, since in them people had the advantage of being with "their own" in the warmth of a windowless igloo).

If we really were serious about the task of evangelizing the existing world, we ought at least to put our minds to the task of discovering it. And even without doing this, whether we want to be a part of it or not, we are. For nobody chooses his very own world any more than he chooses his chromosomes. To be a Christian one must be a man, and it is more than high time that we recognized the kind of men we are today, however non-human we may have been.

The Council began this task with some creaking of bones, but finished off with praiseworthy courage. It is not its fault if it brought to its task a certain dose of naiveté. Of all Christians and all the clergy it was the bishops who were accustomed or caused to be accustomed to living in the most protected regions of the Catholic hinterland. Consequently for the great body of them to speak of the world was to speak from hearsay. Under such conditions, speaking to the world was assuredly well-intentioned but maybe somewhat premature.

I knew a Protestant professor of pastoral theology who said some thirty years ago that if the Church of today wanted to make itself heard by the world, it would first have to get to the point of summing up its creed on a visiting card. In fact, *Gaudium et Spes*, the Council's address to the world, is the most bulky of its documents. It is so profuse that one wonders whether even those who voted for it read it from cover to cover, and of those who did read it how many really understood it. Our old teachers would have told us that there are three formal objects in a scramble here, like the Marx brothers in a parody of a football game, where the one in the rear keeps trying unsuccessfully to edge toward the front. Their first intent, still speaking from the wings, was to try to get up enough courage to look full-face at something that they had previously observed only out of the corner of their eye. The second intention — and here they were most prolific — was to furnish (for the world itself or for the Church? — it is never very clear) a description and an evaluation of this world; unfortunately their good will here is more moving than their factual precision, and especially the precision of criteria. And then they also proposed to proclaim the Gospel to the world. But, although this underlying concern crops up throughout the whole document, like a stubborn cello echoing from the depths of consciousness, it is undeniable that it did not succeed in getting clearly expressed. It would be too much to say that one gets the impression that the Fathers no longer dared to ask anything from the world. We rather have the impression that they did not know too well what to say to it . . . These weaknesses in a composite document, which is incomplete despite its discouraging length (it is always the preachers who don't quite know what they want to say who never finish saying it), do not prevent it from containing some good starting grounds for an attempt at recovery. The very fact that they finally recognized its urgency was perhaps the best one could have anticipated from such an assembly.

Unfortunately, it was not the text's strongest point that

awakened the loudest echo. Up to now it is its only too
obvious weaknesses that have gained adherents, and this
trait has been pushed to the point of caricature.

What has become of the opening to the world that was
proposed to them, that suggested conversion to the world,
for Catholics, at least for those who immediately grabbed
the microphone and monopolized the press? Listening to
them, it is hard not to be reminded of those savages from
remote parts who, seeing a transister, a sanitary fixture or
a packet of contraceptives, suddenly dropped at their door,
can only fall on their knees, firmly believing that the car-
go plane that brought them these wonders could be none
other than the good Lord in person.

To describe the fashion of today in Catholic thought or
what passes for it, people have spoken of a genuflection to
the world. This says much too little. "I do not like this
groveling, this craven groveling, all this rotten slavish
groveling!" said Péguy's God. We must believe that here
at least Catholics have finally heard what God said. But the
groveling in question must be so deep-rooted in their nature
that they could do nothing else, or envision nothing else but
to transfer it to a divinity that is in fact less squeamish
about its worshippers. They even multiply the salaams, pile
up superlatives and go into contortions, trying to outdo
one another! It makes one think of the outrageous phrase,
skillfully pointed up by Canon Martimort in his study on
Bossuet's Gallicanism: "Still hanging at the breasts of the
Roman Church, I prostrate myself at the feet of your Holi-
ness! . . ." Good Lord, what gymnastics! Still hanging at
the breasts of progress, Catholics today endlessly drag
themselves along on their bellies before the more or less
cloven hoofs of all the golden calves with which progress
teems. But what is really extraordinary is that while at

their orisons, they do not hear the enormous burst of laughter gradually growing in the world at the spectacle presented by their maniacal servility. Actually, people stopped taking them seriously long ago. But what else would you want them to do at this sudden and unexpected crawling on all fours by people who turned their backs on you for generations, but hold their sides? Yet, there are sensitive people in the world, and more than Catholics imagine, who not only are not carried away by all this mouldy incense, taken away from God for the sole benefit of their nostrils, but who find the stench of this abject humility nauseating . . .

Catholics of yesterday were incapable of learning any lesson from the world. They are persuaded today that the world, like Mussolini, *ha sempre raggione*. But they forget that the world is not made up only of imbeciles, and that every clearheaded person in it is asking more and more distressing questions. If the Church can still have any meaning for today's world, it is in supposing that she is capable of answering these questions, or, what may be still more important, in helping it finally to ask the real questions. What do we want the world to do with this band of hysterics who find that the crazy idea that there are no problems anymore that the world has not solved or is not about to solve, is enough to plunge them into a state of delirium?

Aggiornamento goes hand in hand with the opening out to the world, and surpasses it. What John XXIII wanted, what the Council had tried to begin — gropingly, as was inevitable, but in the final analysis, forcefully — was the *aggiornamento* of the judicious scribe who searches for the *nova et vetera* in a treasure with which he had become unfamiliar, so occupied was he with keeping it and defending it, like a fierce dragon perched upon his useless hoard. And to respond to the needs of the hour at long last, they had to begin by rediscovering the needs of all time. The *aggiornamento* proposed to us, and which claims to obligate us, consists simply in scrapping the whole idea of tradition in order to fly into the arms of a futurity whose face no one really knows. But the very idea of a history that would approach its term only by abolishing its past is one which the most modern thinkers have discredited. Not for an instant did Einstein think he was nullifying Newton; better than anybody he knew, according to an idea of Pascal's, that he could only perch on his shoulders to try to see farther. If there is anything true in contemporary structuralism, it is that the human mind of our times, as of all the preceding ages, works in inherited frameworks; it can no more escape them than we can jump over our shadows. On a still deeper plane, depth psychology has warned us that people who think they are suppressing their past to free themselves from it, merely repress it in vain. From its refuge within the underground of our personality, it eats away at the roots and makes any genuine development impossible. We must begin by assuming it with frankness so that the real present, in which the future is freely constructed, may begin.

For a stronger reason this is true when, as is the case for Christians, our past contains the unique and definitive revelation of the eternal. Those Catholics who want only to look at the Omega point can preserve Christ only by volatizing him into pure mythology. What he said, what he did, what he is and forever remains, no longer interests them. They keep him only as a tribal symbol, bereft of any particular content; upon it they are ready to stamp just about anything, as long as it is or seems to be new. Do not ask them if they still believe in his divinity: they will answer you proudly that they are above that question. All that concerns them is mankind's future, meaning what our humanity can become since it has reached adulthood, and has taken its destiny into its own hands. (They do not care what that destiny will be: Superman or a monkey with an eye on the tip of his tail, provided that it is new, or at least looks it!)

Jesus, a Jesus who is now completely human since he is *only* human, has no other meaning for them than that of being the promise and the pledge of those mutations which we are told are imminent. Why, rather than any other person from human history, was Jesus chosen for this role? This is what they really do not see! Undoubtedly it is merely force of habit, and with all those who have a phobia about their past this is all the more tyrannical. Yet if there is one trait in Jesus' personality that even the most critical historians agree in acknowledging in him, it is that he lived only for God: the Gospel of the Kingdom was for him what St. Paul felicitously summed up in the formula: "That God may be all in all."

But for these neo-worshippers of the world God is dead. He told them that one cannot serve two masters. They made their choice. The world, Mammon, had them immediately all for itself. As a "new breed" nun said to me recently: "My religion knows only a horizontal dimension now." However, the horizontal dimension alone has never made a religion. What has happened is that religion itself has been sacked, after bargaining away the sacred. But, since in a desacralized Christianity, we have nothing more to do with the Christ of faith, and little more with the Christ of history, in an a-religious world (that is "consecrated" in its very secularness) God obviously quickly becomes the most perfectly meaningless word there is.

After this, let us be no longer surprised to learn that the virgin birth no longer has any meaning for a mankind that is both erotic and contraceptive; that faith in the resurrection ought to be interpreted today as faith in revolution; that words like salvation or redemption can have a sense that is only offensive to the dignity of our contemporaries; that even such a profoundly human biblical term as the Pauline "reconciliation" must be banished ("why?" I asked naively of the excited cleric who taught me this no later than yesterday — "And what are *you* doing about the class struggle?" was his answer) . . . But above all, we must no longer speak about mystery! Such poor people, who think they have discovered the world and who have not yet found out that the mystery that they have chased from religion, or rather which they thought they got rid of along with religion, waits for them there! . . . As Origen said, "the one who has discovered the mystery in the world will no longer be suprised that there is mystery in revelation." But, inversely, those who can no longer bear revelation because of its mysteries, can avoid rediscovering the mystery in the world only by baptizing the final product of their sick imagination with the name "world." Decidedly it was not so easy as they thought for Catholics to return to the world, if the opening out to the world was to be the conversion to reality. But what would it be without that? The bark of Peter taking in water on every side? Obviously in this case Catholicism's only future would have to be none.

TWO

I shall surely be told I am exaggerating, but you must excuse me! If I have not given my references there is not a fact or idea (?) I have not mentioned for which I could not furnish them. "All well and good," you may say, "but this does not represent the whole Church, but only a fraction of it! However much noise it may make, it still can only speak for itself, and what concerns it only involves the people in it . . ." I am more convinced of this than anybody. In the Church today, as in France, there is a loud-mouthed press and the "opinion" it claims to represent or "form" — it would be enough for the masses one day to say what they think for us suddenly to discover the abyss between what the people want and what they are made to say. We still have in the Church (in France and elsewhere) and in the clergy a "bottom" as well as "top," and perhaps it is more in the "bottom" than the "top" that we will find unimpaired the reserves of solid faith and simple good sense. Supposing a genuine consensus could be had (not one of those "polls" where people are only asked questions like: "Are you one of those 'simple people' who do not understand that . . . ?"), we might be surprised, as happened recently in another regard, at the violence of the reaction. But this is precisely what disturbs me and the reason for my speaking out. However pitiful may be the many deformations that parody the needed reforms, their excess is also their cure. The Protestant Churches learned this long ago: negative tendencies find their own extinction in their apparent success. When clerics have lost the faith (and all the more, their morals) their influence soon extinguishes itself, for their lay followers quickly stop going to churches that no longer have anything of the Church about them. At the beginning of this century, an American historian who was born into the Unitarian Church (which had already put into effect all the "reforms" that were supposedly so new and about which we are so dinned in postconciliar Catholicism) wrote in his autobiography: "When we reached adulthood, my brothers and sisters and I, we agreed spontaneously that it was not worth it to waste an hour every Sunday listening to preachers who had nothing to say to us . . ."

However, what happens with people who are not content to give up the faith? They will turn to some form of rigid integralism. And the more violent the negation is, the more distorted will be the reaction.

This is what seems to be the greatest danger to me. And we have already come only too close to this point perhaps, when it does not even occur to us, since we are so absorbed by the tumult of the "contestations" that burn themselves out quite by themselves without our having to relight the stakes. Unfortunately, a good wind of foolishness, like the one blowing at the moment, could easily rekindle the embers; they are not as cold as we might believe.

Until the Council, integralism caused no dismay either by the number or the quality of its representatives. Even the support on which it could rely from high places ought not to cause any illusion. We can see this from what we observed as the wind was changing; with few exceptions its most illustrious advocates scrambled into the first rank of the new Doctors. But the unexpected explosion of a chaotic "progressivism" restored its luck.

What is disturbing is not that so many steering-wheels have turned out to be weathervanes, changing every day. Certainly, little was needed for those who had once made an about-face to make one again with ease. But the most certain effect of their recanting is that for the moment the ship no longer answers orders. Those among them who were informed and in whom a muffled anguish began to ache, would have been quite wrong to imagine that all they had to do was once more to turn about in order to get back the helm. They might possibly succeed in breaking everything that is still in working order—which is not what will put us back on course.

The integralism threatening us today is not one of leaders who have shown their inconsistency. It is one of the masses of deeply wounded good people who, without leaders worthy and capable of leading them, might congeal into a simple hot-tempered refusal to budge. Then perhaps we would stop getting off course and merely sink under. This kind of integralism is on our doorstep.

How should we expect anything else? In a large part of the so-called "Catholic" press, the makeshift guides it has hailed as so many beacons for the new times, agree in presenting to the people of God, as the very expression of integralism, Paul VI's profession of faith—in other words the Creed paraphrased in a language that is both more biblical and more easily understandable to our contemporaries. Could the reaction of such people be anything else than to exclaim: "If that is integralism, that's where we all belong"?

If the good priests who still believe in God and Jesus Christ, and do not have a mistress are all integralists, what good Catholics would not want to close ranks behind them? And if all the faithful who have the nerve to wish that the Mass remain the prayer of the Church (indeed, even a prayer!) rather than a ballyhoo meeting where they are inculcated with political ideas, moral or amoral divagations, and all the other rubbish that today may fill the milky brains of a part of the clergy and their "militants,"—if all these people are treated as integralists, how could the word not become a term of honor?

Nothing is more dangerous than to say again, with its full force, that to believe what the Church has always believed, to do what she has always done, is integralism. For, by dint of hearing it drilled into us, we could indeed come to believe it.

People are moving with great strides. One can say that every progress shouted from the rooftops of a certain "progressivism" has as its primary and most certain effect the spread in depth of a latent integralism which one word too much or a bit of hokum that surpasses the bounds would be enough to precipitate. We shall measure the extent of the havoc when this situation, still fluid today, is no longer so tomorrow. Then, we can say goodbye to our hoped-for reforms! When they were merely in the formative stage they were already too belated. But now what possibilites will be left once the storm is over, the dust of the demolitions caused by the storm has settled, and after the forecast thaw, the ice-pack is found merely to be harder and more compact than ever?

At a high price we have won the freedom without which the Church cannot revive. If today, we only use this freedom to tear down, tomorrow, when it will at least be necessary to try and rebuild, we shall have lost it. And this time, let us not deceive ourselves, it is not the "Roman

Curia" that will be taking it away from us. Not Tom, Dick or Harry, who today are all glorifying in having given it back to us (even though only yesterday they still denied it to us as much as the Curia did!). No, it will be the enraged Christian people. When they see what little we were able to make out of it, they will vomit it out along with ourselves.

"Just a moment!" we shall be told by the optimistic Doctors as they recover all their assurance: "Such a reaction is no threat to us. It has become impossible. And furthermore it would be the definitive ruin of the Church! A new Counter-Reformation, a new encyclical *Pascendi*, would have only the effect of reducing it, maybe forever, to a little group of fanatics, drifting further and further away from the world, bereft of all hope (provided they still had the desire) of ever reaching it!" But, mark well, I am not speaking here of new changes in course (not that they are not still possible, although all that they would be would be harpoons thrown at the water) but one of those jolting reactions of the masses which are most dangerous because they are most incoercible. And if this may seem still improbable to you, it is decidely not merely that you have the wool pulled over your eyes. You have no eyes!

Integralism did not wait for the Council to have its press and its publications. How many copies did they publish? Who read them? Today, how many copies were published of Michel de Saint-Pierre's pot-boiler *Les Nouveaux Prêtres* and its wretched sequel? Its press is quite foolish and repulsively sour, not to mention its reeking of weak-mindedness. It displays for all to see deformities that are more pathological, and despite all these handicaps, it has succeeded in getting a wide circulation. Nor is it particularly far today from the circulation of the press from the other camp, which itself is fast declining these days, despite all its wrangling.

And the worst is that this is not merely a phenomenon of the masses! I have just mentioned Michel de Saint-Pierre. I am very far from confusing him with those pin-heads who were only too happy to get their hands on him. That a man of his caliber, who comes assuredly from a most traditional background, but who also had shown that he was aware of the inevitable adaptations and accepted them goodheartedly, ultimately allowed himself to embark on this galley ship, is already meaningful enough.

If not everyone thinks this example is convincing, what will be said of a letter to the French episcopate which one of my university friends at great pains recently convinced its signers to scrap? It rejected wholesale all the liturgical translations in official use at the moment, and demanded the pure and simple return to the pre-conciliar situation. Were these people "untrained"? Among them there were Catholic university people (of the highest repute today, and rightfully so!) and some sufficiently known to be "leftists."

But the Catholic elite is not completely an intellectual elite. A good test of the reactions of the best Catholics, intellectuals or no, and even the youngest, is the present situation of the religious orders and their recruitment. On the whole, we can point out three cases: those who thought it opportune to put into effect the most radical *aggiornamento,* by running ahead of and if possible beyond all the novelties; those who made an effort to promote realistic reforms, solidly based on tradition, and applied with the least possible shock-effect; and finally those who walled themselves up in a sullen and scornful attitude towards all reform. As surprising as it might at first seem, the first group has not only been run through by series of defrockings, but has practically no new recruits any longer. The second manages to maintain their noviciates for better or worse, but the situation is rather worse than better. Only the third group has a flow of vocations. One of these, especially known for its exacerbated conservatism, no longer knows where to put its novices. People had told me that all these were merely fired-up youths, former colonialists from North Africa, etc. I went to see for myself (taking care to conceal my identity), and I was able to discern that on the whole quite the contrary was true. They were young people who were perfectly sane and normal . . . But, obviously, when one is thinking about spending one's whole life in an institution, we understand that the most generous youths want to have some assurance of stability, and even the brightest among them, in the matter of doctrinal solidity, do not have the means to distinguish between iron-colored reeds and good strong and tempered steel!

But here is the fatal error! Are our "progressivism" and "integralism" enemies? Actually, they are feuding brothers. Quite simply they are what the geometrists call enantiomorphs: they are like a figure and its reverse image in a mirror; everything is opposite, but granting that, everything is substantially the same. Remember Tweedledum and Tweedledee? That is who our friends are!

One aspect that is immediately evident: they live and develop in relationship to one another. Here we find the explanation for that puerile Manicheanism that I described, which was so clearly apparent from the first press reports of the Council. Every display of raving progressivism gives the impetus to a corresponding integralist reaction. Every integralist clamor gives rise to a jubilant "We told you so!" from the "progressivists." Their common ideal

would be to persuade everybody that they alone exist and
that they alone are possible. The tragedy is that little by
little they are succeeding. It is not the tide of destructive
progressivism that is most worrisome. It is the growing po-
larization on these two symmetrical axes that it provokes,
and they only go from one zero to another. Consequently
we are more and more losing sight of the real problems,
and the possibilities of resolving them grow more and more
blurred day by day.

Further, we need not think that progressivism and integralism spend all their time fighting one another. As a
matter of fact, they never stop trying to get together and
to confuse their respective thrusts (which are only apparently divergent) in order to throw a wrench into everything as they wait for it to fall to pieces. I have already
mentioned the singularly revealing bargain with the votes
at the Council, and even more so at the Synod, which continues to a greater extent in the episcopal commissions. The
new eucharistic prayers, the accompanying new prefaces,
and many other essential liturgical reforms that have still
to be made public, were ready for more than a year. Published then, they could have remedied the predicted chaos,
but now they run a strong risk of having no effect on it.
What was the reason for the delay? The roundabout man-
euvers of the Curia, our professional informers will say!
As a matter of fact, the principle reason for it is that it
proved impossible to find a constructive majority in each
vote since the people who wanted to change everything
regularly flew to the assistance of people who wanted nothing changed. And what I say for the liturgy is valid for
everything else.

But still we have not said enough. These same people
have only too often shown themselves capable of jumping

from one side to the other, once it is a question of simply blocking the machine. I saw one prelate vote "no" with his raised hand to the question "Should this text be modified?" Since the result of the voting seemed uncertain the presiding cardinal decided on a second vote with the question inverted ("Should the text in question be kept as is?"). My prelate voted "no" again without hesitation!

We find ourselves, people will say, in the final chapter of Jules Verne's *Mysterious Island*. The port and starboard crews agree to disagree on turning the propellers; each is doing it his own way. But immediately the island does not go forward. It merely turns round and round like a top at the mercy of the currents before bursting and breaking to pieces.

It is true that the integralists, and even more so those good Christians who are tempted today to join ranks wih them, will tell us: "Isn't the only possibility of effectively reacting against the tide of unbelief threatening to swallow us up today, a reinforced orthodoxy?" Our answer first of all must be that there are no degrees to orthodoxy. To believe in the existence of two gods is not twice as orthodox as believing in one. It is a heresy no less serious than believing that there is no God.

Yet this answer is not sufficient. Integralism is a relatively new phenomenon in the history of the Church and in order to overcome the temptation it is necessary to analyze its historical development. Then its collusion with an out-of-joint progressivism contemporary to it will become clear. It becomes manifest that it is not merely a banal form of narrow and intolerant orthodoxy which we have observed at other times in history. It is not enough to say that it does not have the capacity to resist effectively the progressivism opposed to it. Within itself it carries the same germs and in fact engenders progressivism, just as, inversely, progressivism regenerates integralism. It is a circle from which there is no means of escape once we have allowed ourselves to be closed within it. Actually, both can claim the same father: Lamennais, and more generally the whole so-called "traditionalist" school (which in fact has irremediably vitiated the very idea of tradition it claims to uphold). What I feel is that a close-hand examination is needed since it is here and nowhere else that we have the source of the evil or of the chief evils from which we are at the present moment suffering.

We know that in the first stage of his thought, applauded by Joseph de Maistre and Louis de Bonald, Lamennais wished to react against what he called modern "indifference." By this he meant a state of mind engendered by the rationalism and individualism which to him (and to them) seemed to have caused all the excesses of the French revolution, and particularly its attempt to exclude Christianity from society. He believed that any individual who saw no other source of truth but the exercise of his own reason would end up at this point of "indifference." To it he opposed "tradition." But, in the wake of his two predecessors, and particularly Bonald, what was his understanding of the term? For them, the truth, every truth, could be known only by a revelation that was exterior to the individual consciousness. Like the historical revelations of the Old and New Testaments (which they looked on as hardly more than a reduplication of the original revelation, obscured by the process of human history), the depository of this original revelation was society. But we have still to be more specific: they understood society not as something which man, using his reason, could refashion or merely evolve, but as an essentially patriarchal society which the traditionalists supposed was an original creation like revelation. Hence we have not only the so-called "alliance of throne and altar" but also at least the germ of a radical concurrence between the two.

Speaking more profoundly, the horror these thinkers conceived for what they looked upon as the inevitable results of individualistic rationalism, persuaded them that truth is transmitted in society as they saw it as a pure object passed on from hand to hand. The very instant that this truth, and all truth, became the object of an attempt at rational criticism, or quite simply of personal assimilation, it engaged in an irreversible process of disintegration. In their system, authority—an authority of a patriarchal kind —became not only its essential part but also the sole motivating element. Faced with this notion, in order to preserve the truth and that society with which it was united, there was no other attitude possible than a pure and absolute passivity.

Such a system obviously lent itself marvelously to upholding the Restoration of the Ultramontanists. But, if possible, it was still something more. It was a challenge to the Christian spirit rather than merely to the human mind.

At the same period a man called Möhler tried to rediscover authentic tradition. But the excellent analyses in his great book, *The Unity in the Church*, based upon Scripture and the Fathers, traced a very different picture. He showed how, far from being handed on as something external to its transmitters, properly Christian tradition, since it is the tradition of a truth of life, could be transmitted only in life itself — and the most personal — even though it is lived necessarily in fellowship with others. Authority by no means loses its role. But instead of being naturally repressive or

oppressive of the individual consciousness, it became the
pre-eminent educator, guardian, and more than a guardian,
the stimulator of fellowship among persons; it ought therefore to be, if it remains faithful to its role, the natural guide
of an exercise of reason that was never divorced from either
the most intimate or the most open human experience . . .
However, nothing of all this ever seems to have crossed
the mind of Lamennais and his henchmen, any more than
it did the minds of his precursors.

The unrealism of their positions, however, was such that
even governments as chimerical as that of Charles X were
never able to succeed in following them through. Hence the
inevitable conflict that was to lead Lamennais to the most
extraordinary turnabout. From a most insufferably absolutist royalist and Ultramontane position, he turned to an
equally absolutist "populism" and an antiecclesiastical
Christianity. Even a pope as reactionary as Gregory XVI
(and God knows he was) was no-more able to canonize such
a doctrinairism than politicians like Villele or Polignac were
capable of applying it.

It is very revealing to note the occasion of the cleavage
between Lamennais' "ultraroyalism" and the royalty of the
Restoration. It was the most unlikely law that this government ever sanctioned: the law on sacrilege where the pun-
ishment in the gravest cases was the same as for parricides
(the decapitation of the condemned, his head covered with
a black hood, and his right hand cut off before the decapitation). Lamennais and his party were in a state of con-
sternation not because it seemed excessive to them but because they judged it too mild! However, what aroused his
indignation most was that in principle the law would apply
both to the eventual profaners of a Protestant church or
a synagogue as well as to those who profaned a Roman

Catholic church. What he would have wanted was a still more inexorable law, but one that was concerned solely with the defense of the Catholic Church; any protection and even authorization by the State was to be refused to other faiths!

Another cause of conflict with the government of Charles X was to be found in the educational situation. Although the government of the Restoration maintained the theological faculties in the university and the chaplains in the lycees, it refused to embark upon a purge that would have gotten rid of all those minds that were more or less imbued with ideas inherited from the Revolution. Here again the reproach of the Lamennaisians and their disappointment came from their all-or-nothing philosophy, which no government endowed with an ounce of realism could have ever seriously dreamed of putting into practice.

Under these circumstances Lamennais was to have his first contacts with the liberal Catholics of Belgium. Minds more different from his could scarcely be imagined. Their position was inspired by simple pragmatism: their accord with non-Christian liberals in a common effort that was to achieve the independence of Belgium, was proceeding to return to the Church the possibility to develop freely. This possibility was far more realistic than the chimeras of "ultraroyalism." At the moment that this ultraroyalism, for quite opposite reasons, was vacillating in the mind of its *premier danseur*, after a few tergivizations, this reconciliation was to end up by determining an apparent conversion, although in fact, as we must reiterate, it was merely a kind of turning inside out. The idea suddenly germinated in Lamennais' mind—an idea prepared by all he had absorbed from Jean-Jacques Rousseau during his self-taught education—that the patriarchal regime of the old society was

decidedly superannuated. Kings were no longer capable of
expressing the consciousness of peoples. It was for the
people itself, as it reached adulthood, to express directly
the *sensus communis* of universal mankind, since its traditional leaders seemed to have resigned from the role of
being its oracles. Hence his sudden and quite unexpected
exalting of "freedom," first only on the political plane; he
substituted it for authority which he judged to be decidedly defective. But what was this freedom he had in mind?
It was not a rational freedom, which was always confused
with rationalism and individualism, but an instinctive liberty that springs from the consciousness of the masses. In
this way, with a wave of the hand, popular instinct was
substituted for the infallibility previously attributed to
princes (they were stripped of it because they were ill-dis-
posed to following the interpreters of this supposed "tradition"). Never has the adage *Vox populi, vox Dei* been applied more literally than in this second phase of Lamennais'
philosophy. Since Catholic tradition had never been conceived by him as anything other than a mere reviviscence
of the "original tradition" and its heir, the *sensus communis,* it seemed natural and inevitable to him that freed
from the weight of a dead structure, popular sentiment of
itself comes down to a spontaneous accord with Catholic
Christianity. This is the way the accord of "freedom" with
the Church was sealed! Unfortunately it would not be easy
to get the pontifical authority to admit this overturning of
alliances! Since this authority was deeply defiant in the
face of certain presuppositions, which, although they exalted it beyond all measure, bound it to a notion that is as
untraditional as possible, we could not reproach it for reacting ungraciously toward this half-turn to the left that
was suddenly dictated to it in the name of some ambiguous

"freedom" which had sprung like Jack out of his box from a source where one would least expect to find it.

It is only too true that the particularly blind political conservatism of Gregory XVI and his entourage, as well as the reaction of an episcopate that was still basically Gallican and had not digested the idea that it should have its conduct dictated to it in the name of an eccentric ultramontanism, would in no way put the situation to rights. The unrest of the one group (which had been abruptly aggravated by an easily explainable but still stupefying about-face), and the only too perfect opportunity for revenge, bitterly seized upon by the others, found no difficulty in joining forces to bring about the almost instantaneous ruin of the system and its promoter. But, if even one of these factors had not played its part, we must not hide the fact from ourselves that "traditionalism," and its particularly extreme form with Lamennais and his group, in either stage, sooner or later could not avoid expulsion from the Catholic Church as a foreign body. In the last volumes of his *Essay on Indifference* especially, he conceived and described the reabsorption of Catholic tradition into the "original tradition" (whether to make its spokesman the hereditary hierarchy of a patriarchal society, or the hypothetical consciousness of the masses freed from it). This made a complete travesty of traditional Christian faith. The best proof of this is found in the humanitarianism to which the faith would be quickly reduced in his book *Words of a Believer* and in the third and final phase of Lamennais' thought. The Gospel was replaced by a Christianity of the future that had no definite dogma other than the infallibility attributed to the consciousness of the masses.

One peculiarity, which at first sight seems parodoxical, in this last phase of Lamennaisianism deserves further study. This is the exalting of nationalism, first of all Polish nationalism, but soon of all nationalisms. With the collapse of the cult previously vowed to traditional structures and the swift emergence of no less idolatrous populism, we might, on the contrary, have expected the appearance of internationalism. But at this point a transfer of the messianic idea intervenes. It is the "freedom" of all peoples, of the entire mass of humanity, that remains the ultimate objective. But since its old pilots proved faulty, this "freedom" had to find new ones. In place of the "Lord's anointed" we now have the "chosen people." The only thing that does not seem to have been in the forecasts is that far from spontaneously achieving fraternal harmony, these national consciousnesses at white heat entered into rivalries and precipitated the "liberated" peoples into merciless carnage. The worst tyrants of the past would not have dreamed of leading them to such a point . . . But that is another story!

When we dispassionately examine Lamennais' system, through its successive avatars, it is hard to conceive that such an upshot of flagrant absurdities that were reversible at will could ever have been taken seriously, not only by a great part of the clergy and faithful, but especially by its creator himself.

To understand this, we must remember the almost complete collapse of theological culture caused by the Revolution (in France at least) because of its closing down the seminaries and theological faculties, and doing away with the great religious orders. Despite his undeniable genius, in this area Lamennais was completely self-taught, and most of his readers as well. It was only in the last quarter of the century that the situation began to be modified. (Unfortunately the modernism crisis, along with what we must call its savage repression, ended by putting an immediate stop to practically everything!).

But we must also take note of the not only glowing but often brilliant intuitions in Lamennais' writings that surround a central kernel which, unfortunately, is merely an empty shell. The most profound intuition is his truly evangelical sense of the misery and the dignity of the poor and the humble. He expressed this with a power and a pure beauty of language that was worthy of the great prophets and had no equivalent at his time. We must not believe, furthermore, that this sentiment appears only in his "freedom" period. It was already expressed in its full force throughout his period of monarchical and ultramontane absolutism. And it would be wrong to think that in this area Lamennais was unique in his group. The modern democratic historians generally conceal the fact that at the time of the Restoration the only organ that defended universal suffrage was not a republican sheet, nor one of the liberal royalis papers, but Lamennais' *Drapeau blanc,* the paper of the "ultras!" It is quite true that he did this because he was undoubtedly rightly persuaded that the bulk of the people was still deeply attached to the King and to traditional institutions, and that these same institutions had every advantage in relying upon the masses rather than on a nobility that did not yet understand what had happened to it, or on a rich middle-class brought to power by the Revolution and the Empire. Again, we must immediately add that, long before people were talking about socialism, in this same "Ultra" party there were recruited the first defenders of legislation on work and social institutions, which not only sustained the peasantry but uprooted the urban proletariat from the condition of slavery into which early technocracy was on the verge of plunging it. We have to acknowledge that these theoreticians of the absolute power of kings saw them as the born defenders of the people and did not fear the consequences. This was not one of the least reasons for the hatred leveled against them by bourgeois liberalism, whether republican or conservative.

The unfortunate thing is that these generous ideas, ideas that for once are much more realistic than they might seem, are irremediably compromised by Lamennais and his party either with an archaic paternalism or a collectivism of the masses, both of which are equally inimical to the true freedom or the genuine authority that they respectively intend to defend, but, alas, never together.

One other of Lamennais' intuitions is the natural implication of authentic religious developments and the developments of culture. If his applications of this theory never went further than amateurism, he fully understood and was able to say, often felicitously, that Christianity could not live outside culture; it was to live not only in a survival of the cultures in which it was born and grew, but it was also to make an effort to inspire and fecundate their own development instead of lagging behind them. It was to formulate programs which even today seem astonishingly clear-headed; in them he gives a strong outline of the philosophical and scientific renewals that are necessary not only for apologetics but also for theology, and he especially stresses the importance to be accorded to the new historical and philological methods, which seems no less prophetic than his best social ideas. Unfortunately these were merely programs. If they had had the least beginning of a realization at Lamennais' retreat at La Chesnaye, it goes without saying that his system would have been more surely smashed to pieces there than on the rock of Peter!

Similarly, his views about the secular clergy in the renewal of its formation and its manner of living (and even more,
his ideas on the role of the laity, particularly an intellectual elite,—although not solely intellectual—in cooperation
with the clergy) understandably may have appeared elat-
ing to the youth of his time. Since then we have merely
been marking time, presuming that we have even reached
the point at which he had arrived.

The misfortune is that, despite the prestige of a style
that is the most sober and solid of his age, lacking any of
Chateaubriand's bombast, with a musical ring that is perhaps still more enchanting, and despite the romanticism
of a personality that recalls Holderlin's Empedocles, all
of this (which remained in the outline stage) was in the
service or the tow of an unbelievably vapid thought, although its very over-simplification was predisposed to im-
pregnate minds with no more roots than his, in a lasting
way. Although Lamennais' system was consistently being
transformed, it was dead well before the sad end of its author. Up to our own time Lamennaisian influence has left
an indelible mark on French Catholicism, and as a result
of its spread throughout the world, on a considerable part
of modern Catholicism. The ruts into which Lamennais'
thought increasingly sank, and from which it never escaped
(even if it could have followed them all over the map), are
still the same ruts in which both pre- and post-conciliar
Catholicism continues to move. Following an imperturbable
pendular cadence we stubbornly oscillate between progressivism and integralism, persuaded that there is no other
alternative (although this is no alternative at all). In our
own progressivism and integralism, just as in Lamennais'
pseudo-traditionalism and pseudo-liberalism from which
they directly descend, the key pieces are the same as are

the fixtures. The only difference is that the same machine runs at whim sometimes in one direction and sometimes in the other. But its plan of rotation is as invariable as that of the best gyroscope, a plan that nowhere rejoins reality, neither human nor Christian.

In saying this I do not pretend that Lamennais, or more generally the traditionalist school, is the only or even the primary source of our ills. The body of artificial ideas of the traditionalists, and especially the Lamennaisians, whether they are blocked at the first phase of their master or had followed him at least into the second, merely precipitated crystalization. The views they defined and propagated were latent in Catholicism at least since the Counterreformation, especially the excessive role given to authority. They had a false notion of it, looking upon it only as a denial of freedom which itself was identified with its negative forms (freedom *against*, eclipsing freedom *for*).

The ancient theology, that of the Fathers, and even more that of the greatest Schoolmen, acknowledged a twofold "ministry" in the Church, which furthermore was profoundly one: teaching the divine truth and proposing its life-giving mystery in the sacramental celebration. Authority was conceived of as essentially pastoral and did not appear properly distinct from the teaching function. This was due not only to the fact that people had not forgotten then that evangelical truth is the truth of life, but to every notion they had of the law. St. Thomas expressed this with such masterfulness that his statement of it is still one of the most durable parts of his system. According to him in every domain, both natural and supernatural, there is no law worthy of the name unless it is a concrete application to the circumstances of the eternal law that is included in the nature of God and his works. Therefore, the making of just laws and seeing that they are applied is only a consequence of the capacity of teaching the truth. If, as the ancient philosophers thought, the only men worthy of being "politicians" were the sages, *a fortiori* in the Church the function of governing the people of God is merely an appendage to the function of instructing it in the things of God.

From the Middle Ages on, however, there appeared the tendency to change all this. It began by people wishing to find in the Church the three kingly, doctoral and priestly functions attributed to Christ, and outlines appeared that indicated a temptation to absorb the doctoral and priestly functions into the kingly one. Scotism, and the nominalists later on, introduced into their notion of God the deadly concept of *potentia absoluta*, whereby, if he merely wished to do so, God could make evil become good and good evil. In the reaction against the ecclesiastical anarchy of the Reformation, a new ecclesiology, which up to then was still searching, suddenly appeared as the sole ecclesiology possible. This ecclesiology which is perhaps the most typical element of post-Tridentine Catholicism, is practically nothing more than an ecclesiology of "power." Recently, Bellarmine's famous formula has often been quoted to reject it: "The Catholic Church is visible as the Republic of Venice is visible!" But what is quite singular is that what seems to scandalize people the most about this phrase is its assertion of the visibility of the Church. What is scandalous about it, however, is not the assertion that the Church, and particularly its unity, is visible, even if not everything in it is visible, but rather the fact that this visibility is conceived as that of a political power, and what is more, of a power that is the first example of a police dictatorship.

From the moment we find ourselves upon this road, we can indeed declare that the authority is the guardian of tradition. We can even believe it, sincerely wish it and thereby praise it—in fact it has become substituted for tradition. An authority which has no other norm than itself, since it has been made into an absolute, invincibly tends to say: *Stat pro ratione voluntas.* From a servant of the truth, it will become or be on the road to becoming its mistress. The oracle which pronounces and solves according to its own good pleasure is in a fair way to substituting itself for the faithful interpreter.

It is not the tradition of the traditionalists, and even less the *sensus communis* of Lamennais that could provide some counterweight to this quite irrational and despotic notion of authority. As we saw, their tradition as well as that form of authority, by nature absolute, in which they continued to hold it trapped, transmits only a "truth" that is inassimilable. It is only recognized as truth insofar as it is imposed from outside, opposing individual reason. For individual reason to assimilate it would result in its dissolution. And the Lamennaisian *sensus communis*, even when it had rejected the support of authority, was still at this point. If it no longer could be reduced to transmitting a hypothetical "original revelation" that was immutable and undevelopable, its evolvement which was now worshipped like the fallen oracles, is merely in an instinct of the masses, which, like the oracles before it, always has no other rule than an essentially irrational "freedom." The personal spirit is summoned to rally around without argument as it in earlier days prostrated itself before the Juggernaut of deified authority. Indeed, people will talk to us about human progress, an irresistible thing towards which we should converge. But what other authentically human progress could there be than the progress of consciousness, a progress in which the person is basically involved, even if it is true that we cannot fully flower except in a universal fellowship? On the other hand can such a fellowship ever be anything but an unrealizable dream if in its revelation the divine consciousness is not open to ours? And in turn, how can our consciousnesses reach the divine except through the one genuine fellowship of which this revelation has become the source, namely authentic Christian tradition?

Whether, instead of this, we yield without resisting to all mass movements or resign when faced with a simply autocratic authority, our reflex remains basically the same and the results become conjoined. This is not only the weakening and wasting away of any personal life, and also of any collective life (for what can such a collectivity be other than a sum of noughts?). It is either the desiccation or the evaporation of Christian tradition.

The "liberation" effected by these openings out to the world (which are merely a kind of groveling before the ebb and flow of mob psychology) is quite illusory. When the "world," the "people," the "masses," become idols, democracy is nothing more than demagogy. And demagogy is never anything but collective tyranny, even before it gets rid of the tyrants properly so-called, by a reaction that is as unavoidable as it is ineffective. But these tyrants, when their turn comes, can only re-fire anarchy, and we are back on the merry-go-round.

Since integralism (the absolutization of authority or the petrifying of tradition) engenders progressivism, progressivism, which rejects tradition and authority because it identifies them with the image imposed on them by integralism, is a mere extrinsicism. Its "truth" comes from outside, and always remains external to one who accepts it or rather passively submits to it. But if we are afraid to see every stable truth dissolve in the accelerated dissipation of its essentially fleeting truth, even though we exhaust ourselves in vain in pursuing it like an elusive Proteus, our reliance on integralism and its apparent resoluteness is also vain. The arbitrariness of its absolute authority has no more genuine stability than the effervescence in which progressivism loses its strength. And the fixedness of its pseudo-tradition is merely the rigidity of the corpse it has made of living tradition.

Actually, in an integralist or integralizing Catholicism, the truth, which we watch floating away down the stream like a dead tree in progressivism, had already lost its roots and the sap no longer rises. It is now merely a phantom of the truth which, try as we may, we cannot recapture; all the gawks in its entourage are not the ones to prevent its dissolution. When tradition is nothing more than the transmission of formulas or ways of behavior that were supposedly dictated at the beginning or at some other moment by an authority that is completely exterior to the conscience, and when all the conscience can do is accept them without making them its own short of adulterating them, this tradition is in fact nothing but an indurated routine. When the moment comes to reject it, we shall in fact be rejecting only something that we have long ceased to possess.

In this regard I recall an unconsciously revealing reflection made to me some years ago by a priest with whom I was speaking about all the elements of the most truly Catholic tradition that so many Anglicans have recovered and to which they seem much more profoundly attached than Catholics. "But," he replied, "that is valueless since they are not doing it in order to obey the legitimate authority."

In other words, what seemed to him (and to how many others!) to be most proper to Catholicism was not the truth, attested to and upheld by authority, but authority itself, which was thought to be the source of a "truth" that is valueless in itself and has value solely from the decree that sanctions it. With a mentality of this kind people will come, for example, to practice frequent communion only because a pope prescribed it, but had he ordered them to put a ring in their nose they would do so in exactly the same spirit, without bothering in any case to understand the sense of the precept, without giving any internal adherence to it whatsoever, and therefore with no concern for agreeing to it. In the same vein, I shall quote another phrase from another priest who discovered that one of our devout lay friends read the breviary: "Why does he do that? How could he ever have gotten it into his head that he had to do it? "The idea that he could have been doing this simply out of devotion never occurred to him, and had someone suggested it, I am not certain that it would have shocked him. It goes without saying that this priest, a fine and good man, in his own life read the breviary very regularly (and, once again, men who act or rather react like him are legion) but he did so as a *pensum* (was this word not used by the canonists themselves in this regard: *pensum divini officii*?) prescribed by authority, without having the slightest thought that he could, much less that he should, seek edification from it. To put the matter as well as possible, he told himself that he was reciting it "by deputation" as the "official prayer of the Church." But it was up to the Church to make it her prayer if she wanted to (to which apparently the Church hardly gave a thought). All he had to do was passively lend his lips.

Examples of this type are endless. The liturgy was merely a rubrical affair, canon law an obstacle course of incongrous prescriptions (all you were asked to do was to move in and out between the skittles, taking care not to knock any over), moral theology an interminable list of "cases" sorted and classed according to the point of least resistance of the law, and dogma itself was a puzzle whose pieces Denzinger-Bannwart delivered to you all in a jumble: you were to manage with them as best you could; you were required not to drop any of the pieces, but it was of little importance that the finished product made sense or not. Actually, nothing in all of this seemed any longer to make sense. Had we not reached the point of defining (seriously!) mysteries as things that must be believed without our seeking to understand them? In everything all one had to do was to do what one was told, repeat the correct formulas, and reproduce a rubber-stamp mode of behavior. Since the authority, or tradition (that tradition about which the authority could now say: *Io son la tradizione!*), was the source of everything, obedience was "everything," and it it seemed that the ideal obedience was one that was most perfectly unintelligent and most completely uninterested. As one of my old colleagues said to me soon after joining the Oratory: "You can see that you were not always a Catholic. You're much too interested in things like Holy Scripture or the liturgy. Real Catholics don't attach such importance to those things." How right he was! Of course, since the Protestants, and especially since the modernists, Holy Scripture smelled of heresy. As much could not be said of the liturgy, but like Scripture, if one gave too much attention to the liturgy in a manner that was not exclusively rubrical, it betrayed only too clearly a notion, or rather an application of the Christian religion that had nothing in common with "real Catholicism." Understand by this, naturally, the Catholicism of people who were Catholics simply because their parents were before them, and for whom the problem was to keep it intact; to do this they should have as little to do with it as possible—live in it, yes, but subsist from it, certainly not!

For "good Catholics" could be devout and even fervent people. Their training in passive obedience and in the equally passive acceptance of everything labeled "traditional" combined easily with a kind of moral stoicism that was narrow perhaps, but respectable if not admirable. With people of a more mystical bent this was enlivened by devotions (devotions not devotion). They were like the premiums of the system which in small measure relieved its dryness and emptiness by furnishing them with a sentimental religiosity. There was the Sacred Heart, Our Lady of Lourdes (or Fatima), the good St. Joseph, the Baby Jesus, the Little Flower, or simply, for more prosaic souls, St. Anthony of Padua or St. Rita. Souls in mourning might prefer the souls in purgatory. The different scapulars were particularly practical because they guaranteed you every wish and every protection without your having to contract any burdensome obligations, not even the obligation to think about them: it was enough that you had them on.

A new devotion, the mysticism of incorporation in Christ, propagated by Benedictines like Dom Marmion or Dom Vonier, was not positively ruled out. The Paulinism of both of them was a questionable recommendation, but the pieces of "St. Thomas toast" that Dom Thibaut buttered for Dom Marion's work and the more innate Thomism of Dom Vonier protected them from frontal attack. The good judges, however, like the good priest that reviewed both of them for *Les Etudes* on the eve of the war, pointed out that they did contain a threat of quietism which more traditional (*sic*) devotions did not present. They might be tolerated with the Benedictines or with artistic people, and intellectual converts who haunt the churches, but we must be watchful lest such rather fanciful types of spirituality spread among the masses of the fanciful. For a seminarian, this could be a blameworthy affectation that ought positively be discouraged, like buying a "Gothic" chasuble for his first mass.

If Scripture especially, but also the liturgy, were unable to nourish a reliable spirituality, and had to be strictly limited to a merely decorative role (the first as sacred eloquence, the second as the external worship of the Church), it was because they deviated from pure abstraction which makes sound doctrine, and from the psychological training which is everything to a solid piety. Both lent themselves to being interlarded with emotion by the tried and true devotions, in order to facilitate their ingestion. But in the biblical and liturgical texts, people got wind of a vitalism that they judged to be immanentistic, as with Newman and Blondel. It was difficult to condemn, but it would be more than imprudent to let it infect "real Catholics." That would have done away with its rigidity, which, as was thought, was its whole strength. If the spirituality of incorporation in Christ was to be held firmly by the leash, and at the very most conceded to groups that were esoteric and archaizing, the devotion to the Holy Spirit was called nonsensical by the licensed theologians. An incontestable master of the most reliable Thomism (since it was what was taught at the Gregorianum, even if it was not completely St. Thomas' system), piled up article after article and book after book to demonstrate that the Holy Spirit had nothing to do with the presence of grace in us. His name was connected with and he was certainly not overly inclined to optimism in this regard.

But our new "theologies of the salvation of unbelievers" are from the outset set apart from these traditional views, although they take refuge behind them through a total reversal of viewpoint. Now people want to draw from Christian revelation itself a theology of salvation that extends it to all men, without their needing any longer to have faith in this revelation, nor, evidently, even to know it. The innumerable systems worked out with this aim in mind since the beginning of the century need not be explained here. Let us say only that they all distinguish themselves by the same Byzantinism, the same arbitrary manipulations of all the traditional notions, and finally the same verbalism that characterized the only kind of theology that was judged to be orthodox at this period. The esoteric sense that they came to give to such transparent expressions as "desire for baptism" or "belonging to the Catholic Church" is so far from the natural sense of the words that only people who had long yielded to this kind of intellectual gymnastics could be comfortable with it. On everyone else, the reading of these speculations has the irresistible effect of nonsense bordering on pure buffoonery. But when one is accustomed to calling black white and white black this all seems perfectly natural and one is astonished at the astonishment of others!

On the other hand, it is well understood that the type of theology we have described tends to make these systems proliferate. Its basic notion of a totally unconscious supernatural, like an external veneer on human reality, succeeded in making the statements of faith so arbitrarily gratuitous and so empty of any vitality that to make them a condition of salvation would unfairly make God the Sav-

ior appear to be a nightmarish divinity: a way out had
to be found at any price. Yet, once this door was opened, it
was unavoidable that a system which was merely wind any-
way should blow out through it and that soon nothing
would be left.

The basic error of these theories of salvation is that they
have nothing to do with salvation in the Christian sense
of the word. From the start, they suppose that a non-
Christian man is already saved and consider him to be the
normal man. But if he were, there would never have been
need for Christianity. "I have not come to call the righteous, but sinners," Christ said. All these theories are merely theologies of the salvation of the righteous who, precisely
if they are already righteous (however they may have become so—which remains God's secret if it was not by the
preaching of the Gospel), do not need to be saved because
they already are.

The return effect on the theology that engendered these
monsters is necessarily annihilating. What is more serious,
and we are discovering it today even though we could easily
have long foreseen it, is that since the theology in question
had itself declared the sole "true theology," people have
come to believe that really traditional Christianity should
be thrown out along with it.

If faith, baptism, and the Church are "necessary for salvation" only in the sense that they are necessary for those
alone who know and accept the superstructure of artificial
dogmatism placed by their side, it goes without saying, or
seems to, that this necessity is non-existent since it is obviously completely artificial. If explicit faith, actual use of
the sacraments, and belonging to the Catholic Church in a
visible, conscious and willed way, bring us nothing for salvation that we do not already have without them, how

grace in Scripture or the Fathers only by an appropriation, in which we should see nothing else but a kind of poetical fiction, bereft of any real content by the sacrosanct doctrine of the undifferentiated community of all the *ad extra* actions in the three persons of the Trinity. But he had not said enough: in good doctrine grace relates to the divine essence, and not to the persons, from the point of view of its efficient causality. Here we have our finger right at the heart of the matter: if this Catholicism (the only "real" Catholicism, remember) in the last analysis had nothing to do with our "personal religion" (despite the timid but courageous defense of this expression by another noted Jesuit), it is because it also had no idea about the life of the persons in God. Did not St. Thomas tell us this? Properly speaking, we are not the sons of the Father, but of the Trinity, without distinguishing the persons, which is to say that we are the sons of the divine essence.

It is true that when doctrine is reduced to this kind of abstraction, its formulas no longer have much nutrient value. The acceptance only of formulas of this type, which were declared to be the only ones sanctioned or sanctionable by authority, created a kind of ideal *shibboleth*. The less people saw what all that could mean, the easier it would be to subscribe to it, without the possibilty of argument or reflection.

But could it be maintained that assent to formulas of this kind was "necessary for salvation"? Great care was taken to maintain it in words, but there was a tendency towards, or better an anticipation of a complete draining off of the natural sense of these words. As a result, it would always be possible to make more refinements upon the Byzantinism of a super-orthodoxy. From the moment that it was taken as effectively "necessary for salvation" only by those who were able to know it, understand it, or at least understand that they should adhere to it without seeking to understand anything in it, they need no longer be scrupulous or embarrassed about further rarefying its quintessence.

Actually, parallel to the arrival of this super-orthodoxy, whose growing extrinsicism seemed in its own eyes to be the guarantee of its purity, we see appearing and growing before our eyes a curious "theology of unbelievers." It is quite characteristic that the same thinkers produced both simultaneously. The name of Cardinal Billot can serve as a patron for both, and that says everything.

What is this theology, and above all what is this "salvation of unbelievers?" In the good old days, it was always believed that the unbelievers normally had to come to salvation through the preaching of the Gospel. Even the most rigoristic theologians, like St. Augustine after the Pélagian controversy, admitted that if the unbelievers were unable to hear the Gospel preached, or heard it only in a situation where they could not understand it, God, in his infinate mercy and power could use other means, known only to him, to touch their hearts and convert them. More precisely, if there were "pagans," or even atheists whose virtues were authentic, who were seekers of truth, and for a stronger reason seekers of God, there was every reason to think that this was the case and that they could certainly be saved. Inversely, many apparent Christians, who were inwardly unfaithful to their external profession of faith, would not be. "There are many who seem to be outside (the City of God) and whom we shall ultimately find there, just as there are many who seem to be already there and who, in the last analysis, will show that they do not belong to it": this was St. Augustine's judgment on this point, could the Church and everything connected with her (especially once we concentrate our attention exclusively on what people have tagged on to her, and which is so far from being essential to her that it is merely a caricatural deformation) be anything else but an enormous dead weight? If that is the case, people who reject it, whether in part like the Protestants or completely like the modern atheists, or people who never heard of it like the pagans, seem obviously to be in a much better position than Catholics.

How could they still envision propagating their faith? What is the use of running around the whole world to make one proselyte, if it is true that all we would be doing in these circumstances would be making one slave more of so many truncheons, prohibitions, rubrics, casuist subtleties, canonical red-tape, and finally of a still-born tradition and a simply paralyzing authority?

But also in these circumstances, why remain a Catholic at all? Belonging to this type of Catholicism, which is thoroughly extrinsic to the life of the person, and where the emphasis is only on all the historical accretions that have become so oppressive, can only be justified by equally extrinsic motives. It is therefore no accident if the theology of our "real Catholics" has developed such a close alliance with the nationalism of *Action française*, that it long appeared to be inseparable from it. Nor, let us add, is it an accident if, when a pope like Pius XI saw that the moment had come to do away with this deadly ambiguity and to break the ties, after a short skid into a "primacy of the spiritual" (which, in accordance with their own principles, could no longer in fact be anything but a primacy of the abstract and the unreal), Marxism seemed to have come in the nick of time as the hope of an incarnational replacement.

This is the exact equivalent of what happened with Lamennais. Catholicism is reduced to an ideology, conceived completely as a justification, or else a tradition that is itself boiled down to a conservatory of dead formulas, or else (or including!) a deified authority, and the ideology will seek in return its own canonization by the authority. Having lost the truly human and truly supernatural corporeity of the authentic life tradition of the Catholic Church, this Catholicism can subsist humanly only as a parasite either on the temporal institutions of the past or on the mass movements that seem pregnant with the future. Since it is nothing but a skeleton of frigid concepts, it can only live curled up like its incubus over an old human society; to its conservative nationalism it offers a questionable promise of immortality. Otherwise, when this will have proved vain, drunk with its sudden unfocused freedom, it will hasten to become incarnate in the arms of earthly messianism. This latter will only be able to do with this "extra soul" what it proposes to it. It will not work, for want of kicking aside this preposterous succubus, after having unscrupulously gotten all possible advantages out of an ephemeral flirtation which it is the first to mock. But, without the corpse of the dead societies that had to be abandoned willy-nilly, Marxism will have lured for a time, with the vain hope of a reincarnation in the "masses," this phantom of the Roman empire weeping over in its tomb. Has the Catholicism about which we are speaking ever actually been anything else? The idea of Gibbon to which we have just alluded may be unjust, not only as regards the Catholic Church, but also in regard to the papacy at which its whip was directed. On the other hand, we must acknowledge that it is striking directly out at a Catholicism identified with absolute power, the sole source of all truth, which is thought to preserve intact the traditional City of God, but which in fact tended to substitute for it a very human Tower of Babel; when one of the two is lacking, it can only fly to the other as it begins to rise in its place.

Even when these extremes are not reached, it is too characteristic of the Catholics about whom I speak, whether integralists or the reversed and progressive side of the same glove, that they cannot envision a Catholicism that is not political; whether Right, Left or Center, it must be first of all political. I am the first one to believe that Catholic Christianity, as Father Walgrave has just demonstrated in his book, *Cosmos, Person and Society*, is the natural inspiration of politics in the great Aristotelian sense of the word. This is to say that it it the most reliable and most powerful motivating force of a constant rebuilding of human societies, fully rooted in the earth and naturally opened to heaven (not the heaven of fixed ideas, nor that of the falling stars, but the heaven of the Christian God). But first of all it cannot be identified with this building process itself. It is never anything else but its earthly reverberation, however necessary or inevitable that may be. For an even stronger reason it cannot curl up with what we call "politics" today, but which is merely the regime of the various parties, or the dictatorship of one of them. On the contrary, this *caput mortuum* of bloodless abstractions, that is the Catholicism about which I am speaking, is a parasite which took root in the body of the Church only after having emptied it of its substance; it is constantly looking for additional incarnations in the political parties where it hopes, always in vain, to find the substance of humanity which it lacks. At certain times it will attempt to provide itself with a party of this type, which would actually belong to it. But it would only succeed in creating a phantom party, and if it were unable to extricate itself from it, it would be breathing in stagnant waters of the quagmires of a systematic opposition to progress, as represented by all these modern political "centers." If it seeks to be stimulated by violence—the customary resort of those wishful supermen who in fact are powerless—it instinctively goes toward some form of totalitarianism, of either the Left or the Right. Totalitarianism, actually, is related to it by birth. Charles Maurras' Comtism, like Marxism-Leninism, with its Stalinist or neo-Stalinist offspring, are merely secularizations of the earthly Messianism of the Grand Inquisitor. Did not Comte admit this ingenuously in his unbelievable but perfectly logical letter to the General of the Jesuits (*Civiltà cattolica*, old style, a Metternich style Catholicism)? For his part, Lenin had said things on the subject which I should prefer not to repeat. This book will make me enough enemies without that!

And even if it does not become entirely absorbed in such political systems, the Catholicism I have in mind feels itself, and shows itself politically, to be a caste, a race or a class. We have been able to say of Judaism that its spiritual evolution brought it little by little from an ethnic clan to a religious community. On the contrary, this Catholicism can only regress from a Church to a clan. The Augustinian and Gregorian ecclesiastical ideal (*in necessariis unitas, in dubiis libertas, in omnibus caritas*) inspires it only with an insuperable terror. It feels too strongly that with it it would disappear into thin air. What it needs is a uniformity imposed from outside and from on high. And this uniformity will never be anything but the uniformity of a particular group, a particular school, a narrow community withdrawn into itself which aspires to be Catholic, i.e. universal, only by suppressing or at the very least ignoring everything that is not itself. For this Catholicism in name, the only true catholicity, which is the living unity of fellowship in supernatural love, will have the effect of being a Protestant ideal. Since it desires to be anti-Protestantism, anti-Modernism or anti-Progressivism, it will in fact never be, as Möhler discovered even before Khomyakov, anything but an individualism of a clan or, in the extreme, of one man (totemized rather than divinized) opposed to the individualism of everyone. It will only be able to allow one sacred language, one liturgical tradition (forever fixed by authority), one theology (not Thomistic, despite its claims, but at the very most "John-of-St.-Thomistic"), one canon law (integrally codified), etc. The riches in the thought of the Fathers, which are so concordant, but also so manifold and so open, are always suspect to it. The fullness of the Holy Scripture, which is so profoundly one, but also so broad and deep like the universe itself, would suffocate it; it forbids its access to everyone and carefully abstains from taking anything from it other than a few *probatur ex Scriptura's*, isolated from their context, or a few rhetorical festoons, like those which the latter pagans continued to borrow from a mythology in which they had long since ceased to believe.

Any arrival of newcomers to this "sealed household" will appear as a threat to its claustration. Converts can only be admitted (even still!) if they improve upon the narrow-mindedness of those who consider themselves the sole legitimate owners and occupants. And swear as they will that the world from which they came does not count, does not exist, the very fact that they came from it will make them "unsafe." They can be used, prudently of course, for *ad extra* polemics, or, preferably, limited to being exhibited *ad intra* like hunting trophies, comforting those who might have some doubt about those invisible "victories" that fill their ears, but care will be taken to do this only after they have been eviscerated and stuffed with straw. Even after all that, they will never be trusted. They will remain interlopers in a strictly segregationist club. They can lend themselves to all the circumcisions that might be wanted, but in vain. Since they were born outside the seraglio, even a complete castration would not succeed in reassuring our friends to the point of opening all the secret passageways to them.

However, when the moment comes — and it is impossible for it not to come — when the lack of air gets so stifling, they will have to be resigned to breaking open the door for lack of windows. What will happen? The house, which seemed to have been made of iron, on a rock foundation, will suddenly reveal the brittle clay and the shifting sands upon which it was built.

Since, as we know, the world is already saved by the Gospel, it is the Gospel that will be chucked in order to come back into the world. In fact, for quite a long time they have merely been retaining its shadow. There will be no difficulty in swearing to the world that they have no wish (even though out of an old habit they may still speak of a "mission") to conquer it for the Church, but only to assist it in becoming aware of the supernatural values it already possesses. Should the world shake with laughter at this nonsensical offer, all they will then do is announce that the sole message the Church still has for it is the empty consolation by which they justify their disinclination to evangelize it, after having made any evangelization impossible by their desiccation of the Gospel for their own use. What a rapid deterioration we have witnessed these past thirty years in the themes of evangelization! The Ca-

tholic Action movement of the thirties wanted "conquest."
With the priest-workers all that was wanted was "presence."
After the war it had already drawn back to "witness."
Today, this presence is so anxious to be forgotten about,
to be immersed in all the world's ebbs and flows, that we
no longer see what makes it any different from absence.

What has happened is that the *de facto* particularism of
integralist or integralizing Catholicism had already completely lost the Gospel's transcendence from sight, and re-
fuses to admit its immanence. Since it no longer thought
of itself as anything but a sect, which was unable to believe
itself the true sect except by denying and forgetting all the
others, it had already lost the sense of the gifts it had received as a mandate for the world. These were no longer
graces given to it primarily, but simply possessions; they
were tribal symbols that it guarded jealously, but as its
own possession that it was reluctant to share. It could look
down on those who did not have these fetishes, or else
excuse them, depending on its temperament. It was not at
all keen on the point that others may have the same rights
and the same access to them. Once again, however, it did
not really have access to them all: what seemed sacred
to it also seemed equally untouchable.

The only mission that it could still envision was conceived,
quite typically, only in terms of "conquest," and not of
sharing. But it had only to go out of its windowless house
for the mockery of such a project to be obvious. Hence
its successive withdrawals. The idea of "witnessing" could
have opened the way if the witness had not been so unconsciously, but exclusively, full of himself. Hence that
"presence" which tried to last for a while, not only without
even daring to make any conditions, but without having
anything to propose. The end result has been this absence

about which we have spoken, the final swoon of an external
Catholicism, which cannot turn back in order to open out
to the world without falling back into its essential nothingness. We open ourselves to the world, in principle, to announce the Gospel, but once we are open, we perceive that
we have nothing more to say to it, for all we have preserved
from the Gospel is an empty crust.

After all that, since they have long given up the idea
of converting the world (simply because they have lost any
desire to convert themselves to the Gospel that they retained without living it) we should not be surprised that
Catholics who go finally out to the world allow themselves
merely to become caught by it like flies on fly-paper.

THREE

When all is said and done, this history of Catholics, whether yesterday's (or tomorrow's) integralists or today's progressivists, that we have been trying to retrace and explain, is rather banal. It is the story of sons of families, who are too well brought up, whose education has been too protective. When the day comes to give them free rein, they see no other possible use of their freedom than to run to the nearest place of ill repute . . . where, naturally, they immediately catch the pox. I apologize for the vulgarity of the comparison, but it corresponds exactly with the vulgarity of this shabby history.

If this is the situation, what hopes do we have of getting out of it? The first one, which is still negative, is that people finally open their eyes and come to understand that the laughable conflict between integralists and progressivists has no more interest for the future of the Church than a slapstick war, although it is much less entertaining.

Putting this false problem aside, we must go back to the source of the evil. If, as we believe, it proceeds entirely from a corruption of the very sense of authority and tradition (and correlatively of Christian freedom), this should be our point of focus. To oppose the principles of tradition and renewal, or authority and freedom, is to show that we have completely lost the Christian sense of these ideas.

As Möhler showed so well, at the very moment the "traditionalists" and the Lamennaisians were propagating their inept theories, since Christian truth is the truth of life (a life that is essentially supernatural, although it develops through total impregnation of life plain and simple) Christian tradition can only be propagated in the entire life and the personal life of those who open themselves to its truth. A tradition that would be merely the exterior transmission of ready-made formulas and ways of behavior imposed by mere conformism has nothing in common with it.

The inspired expression of the Word of God in Holy Scripture is the kernel, or better the heart, of this tradition. Once people pose a problem like that of Scripture and tradition, understanding by this not only two distinct objects, but two separate ones, they are distorting it. Scripture itself is the central element of tradition, but it is also part of it. Inversely, a Christian tradition isolated from Scripture would be a body from which the essential organs had been removed. By its nature, which flows from its origin, Scripture is not only incomprehensible but also devitalized as soon as it is isolated from the tradition of living truth in which it originated and in which alone it can be preserved as a Word of Life.

On the other hand, in its continuing life, as Newman showed better than anyone in a justly famous page from his *Prophetical Office of the Church*, tradition is presented under a twofold aspect which is equally indissociable. There is what is called the prophetic tradition and the episcopal tradition. This latter corresponds exactly to what most modern theologians have the habit of calling the magisterium. But it is possible to think that Newman's formula is better, for it emphasizes that the magisterium itself can no more be isolated from tradition than Scripture is.

The prophetic tradition remains the basic element, for it is the life of truth in the whole body of the Church. But since this body exists only in concrete persons, it comes down to saying that tradition is the truth lived by all Christians, each individually, and all together. For it is essential to their life, as it is for the truth from which this life proceeds, that it be a life in fellowship, and more precisely a life in the supernatural love that the Holy Spirit unceasingly spreads in our hearts. In this life of truth, each has his part, in proportion to his lights, nature and grace, and above all in proportion to his faithfulness to grace. It lives in the heart of the humblest faithful as well as in the heart of the most profound theologians. And in order to live it as we should, everyone needs one another. The simple will be unable to defend their faith, or even explain it when they need to, without the help of the most learned. But the speculations of these learned men will be lost in the clouds if they do not unceasingly return to the faith of the simplest people and to its spontaneous expressions in everyday life.

Nevertheless, this life of truth, received in frail, fallible and sinful spirits, even with all the helps of grace, grows only in a kind of mixed way. Its developments need unceasingly to be sorted out, verified and brought down to essentials. It is here that the episcopal tradition intervenes. It is not a tradition that is different from prophetic tradition, and it is not enough to say that it plunged into it with all its roots: it is completely immersed in it and belongs to it. But since the bishops received the responsibility for the development of the whole body in the unity of divine love, they have also received a special grace: that of judging, evaluating and authenticating the faithful expressions of tradition. Hence, not only their power, when controversies arise, to give solemn definitions which obligate the assent of everyone, (although in a more habitual than *ordinary* way), but also their guidance in the formulation of these expressions, as well as supplying other expressions, especially by sanctioning the forms of worship in which the faith of all must be unceasingly regenerated at its source. For this the bishops are in no way endowed with any quasi-oracular power. They are not favored with the inspiration, in the strict sense, which the apostles had. To form their judgments, they must use human means which are within the reach of all Christians: above all the study of Holy Scripture in the light of the whole of tradition. It is even quite possible that people other than they, in particularly decisive circumstances as well as in daily life, might discover renewed expressions of the truth that is always the same, which the Church needs. But it belongs to them as their task and their particular grace to recognize, and canonize (i.e. authenticate) these expressions in the presence of the faithful, whether they are their own or not . . .

Newman's views, like Möhler's, are only a striking summation of everything that the Catholic Christian tradition has always said of itself, from the time of the Fathers, and particularly at that time which was the most creative in the history of the Church, after the apostolic period.

If this is the case, we see immediately how a mere "power" ecclesiology, slipping fatally into the blasphemous chimera of absolute power on the part of one or several persons, is quite un-Catholic. But we also immediately see how little Catholic are the attempts or the temptations to wrench Scripture out of the living context of tradition, or to emancipate tradition from the authority of the lawful pastors.

Their authority is in no way a mere delegation by the body which can always be revoked. It is a permanent gift of the Head, Christ, to his body and it must be received as coming from him. But it must never be exercised in a way that would curb life, or extenuate freedom, and the bursts of spontaneity. For a stronger reason, it could not function separately in isolation. It can never act except as something immersed in the body itself, attentive to all the gifts of the Spirit that are manifested here, but attentive also to distinguishing them from their ever-possible counterfeits. It must be watchful to stimulate, point out, and proclaim the value of all that is authentic, but also, when necessary, to correct, to thwart, and, if this regrettable but sometimes unavoidable extreme is necessary, to condemn anything that may be a corruption or a deviation. Again, in this case, authority must be attentive not to put out the still-smoking wick, to distinguish carefully what truth may be mingled with error, and to lay claim to it.

Reciprocally, every Christian—and the theologians as much and more than the rest, since they have the means that are not given to everyone—must also, to the extent of his capabilities, be attentive to all the gifts of his brothers and not only of those who are alive today, but to the experience of all who preceded them in the faith and have handed it down to them. Moreover, every Christian must always return to the basic source, to the central expressions of the Gospel throughout the whole of inspired Scripture, as it is given to him in the heart of the continual experience of the living and praying faith which is the traditional liturgy. There particularly, but also in all circumstances, with an intelligent docility that is sympathetic to what he is taught, he must let himself be guided by the lead of the pastors which the Sovereign Shepherd,

Christ himself, appointed to watch over the whole flock. He will be especially attentive to the definitions or solemn teachings to which the magisterium has given its whole authority. But he will not have the puerile reaction of believing that he must respect only those decisions formulated under the cover of infallibility. Even if, and especially *because* he is always seeking to understand in a living and therefore intensely personal way the entire truth that the whole Church, of which he is an integral part, is proposing to him, he will know that in every doctrinal directive of authority, even if it is always perfectible and even if it may be tainted with some human error, there is something there for him. It is a grace of light that he can receive only in a spirit of deference in regard to those who have received, along with a responsibility he does not have, special graces that he also does not have. If he has difficulties, and if he has any solid motives for thinking they are real, he will bring them to their attention, and if necessary will not hesitate to insist, with a son's boldness, that his difficulties be given a fitting hearing. But he will always keep in mind that he is only one member in a body which is greater than he, that other members have responsibilities that are not his, that to weaken their authority is as much as weakening the unity of the entire body, and also that the truth of the Gospel can neither be found nor even less subsist outside the unity and unanimity of supernatural love.

These are indeed onerous conditions. They are exacting, but they are the price of the true freedom of the children of God, the sole positive liberty, and the only freedom that is a freedom to build, and to progress in love; it is not simply the freedom to destroy, to curl up into one's own shell, or inversely, to collapse into chaos and nothingness.

But for their part, the leaders must realize that they cannot be faithful shepherds if they do not accept still more radical exigencies for themselves. The first is to be convinced that the truth of the Gospel, of which they are not only the primary witnesses but the responsible guardians and propagators, is not accessible to them in a different way or at a lesser price than it is to other Christians. They are not the successors of the apostles in the sense that they enjoy a special inspiration similar to theirs, but in the sense that they are assisted by the Holy Spirit in preserving and developing what the apostles taught, by first of all using to the maximum all the means available to everyone in the Church, and by having the humility to welcome what others, more gifted naturally or supernaturally than they, can get from them. If they do not do this, they will not simply be lukewarm or dull-sighted Christians, but prevaricators. They are the born doctors of the Church because they are her shepherds. But, reciprocally, they will be faithful shepherds only if they are concerned truly with being teachers. And this is not a simple gift that they received *ex officio* but a task to perform, a work to agree to, with all its exigencies, which are not solely intellectual, although in the highest sense of the word they are. The professional theologians are certainly there to help them, but they can no more substitute themselves for the bishops than the bishops can do without them.

But again, the bishops must not be autocrats, but guides, stimulators and leaders informed about the whole life of their flock. They must know this life, be interested in it, become part of it, and be the first to live it. To say, as did the old theologians, that the bishops are in a state of acquired perfection in no way means that they need have no concern about life, but that they must always feel themselves under God's judgment if they do not do all in their power, with help from heaven, to be perfect Christians, which means that they must be men of God, men entirely given over to supernatural charity and its merciless exigencies.

This does not mean by any means that they must simply be followers, ready to give their blessing to everything indifferently. They are servants, but servants of Christ for the good of their brothers. This means that they cannot abdicate their responsibilities. They are the ones to make the final decisions, even if they must never be lured by the convenient illusion that no initiative could be good unless the idea had come to them first . . .

But above all they are responsible for the unity of the Church: first of all, the unity of the particular Church entrusted to them, then its unity with all the Churches under the supreme responsibility of the bishop who is Peter's successor. They must always remember that this unity is not uniformity, it is not simply an outward conformity obtained by decree. It is the unity of charity, the unity of a great concert, of a full symphony of which they are to be the conductors, where they must be concerned that each voice be heard, but in its place and in accordance with its proper value, recalling that the only definitive choir-master is Christ himself. They are simply his representatives, and the breath that must pass through all the mouths, and be first of all in all the hearts, is that of the Spirit of whom they are merely one of the instruments . . .

Who will not say to all of this: "But that's exactly what we want!"? Unfortunately, the desire is not everything. We must still desire the means. Before concluding with a few reflections on this subject (they may be inopportune, but they are certainly not unreal), there is still something else to be said.

Up to now all we have done is describe the ideal life of the Church in its interior aspect. This assuredly is basic. What would a Church have to bring to the world, if it had no interior life, no life proper to it, even though it is not its life nor ours, but the life of Christ and of his Spirit in us? However, life, and the gifts of life the Church has received, are not for her, if we mean by that her present members, but for the world. In the time between Pentecost and the Parousia the Church is in an essentially missionary situation. Again, on this point everybody today is in agreement. Unfortunately, despite everything that is said and written about this, we may wonder if the Church was in the past ever as un-missionary-minded as she is today. Blocked by the absurd conflict, which once again is only a pseudo-conflict, between integralists and progressivists, her mission has come to a halt and will stay there as long as we do not get out of this deadly circle. How can the integralists, who turn their back to the world, ever be missionaries? And how can the progressivists, who are open to the world, but who are unaware of having anything to bring to it, be anything more?

Finally we have to dispel these consoling or rather anesthetizing illusions. There is no "salvation without the Gospel," no "anonymous Christianity," no "implicit Church." These are so many chimeras that worn-out Christians have invented to dispense themselves from working at a task that they are obliged to perform even though they think they have lost the means to do so.

For the world to be saved, in the evangelical sense of the word, we have first to believe that it needs to be. We must then believe not that *we* have the means but that God has them, since through no merit of our own he revealed them

to us, and that he has entrusted them to us. We do not
believe any of that any more, and one of the Byzantine
tasks to which contemporary theology devotes itself by
preference, is to convince us that despite the declarations
of the Gospel or the apostles which are most clear on this
point, we need not worry about it. As long as we persist in
this attitude, not only will the world not be evangelized,
but even salvation itself will elude us. The desacralized
Christianity of which we dream is a Christianity where God
no longer manifests himself; a Christianity which no longer
wishes to be a religion is a Christianity deserted by God;
a Christianity without God is no longer Christianity. We
can turn the thing over and look at all of its angles and
vie with our pharisaical subtleties in its regard. God knows
we have been doing that long enough! We shall not be
successful.

I do not think I have to dwell any longer on this subject:
everything that ought to be said about it, today as always,
in my opinion has already been said much better than I
could say it, by a simple woman who is one of the rare
apostles of our time, and whom I think, *salvo meliore judicio*,
the Church might one day canonize. I am speaking of
Madeleine Delbrel and her unpretentious book: *We, People
of the Streets*. It is the most invigorating reading that could
be recommended at the present time.

I do not think anyone has lived more courageously, more
integrally, this true opening out to the world that consists
in knowing it because one has lived fully in the world with
one's heart and eyes fully open. But at the same time, and
without any contradiction because this woman knew how
to see it (and love it in the true evangelical sense of the
word) better than anyone, she never succumbed for an instant to the temptation to believe that the world was

already saved and all one had to do was to rejoice with it. But this was also because for her the Gospel of Christ was not simply the expression of the particular experience of a little group, nor was the Church simply this little group with its qualities and defects, its good sides and its taints. She accepted the Gospel and the Church of Christ and she lived them as a gift of God. She was more aware than anyone how much "humanity" there was in the Church, but she no less believed that the Church is the Bride and the Body of Christ himself. She was no professional exegete, but she knew all the historical problems and particular difficulties posed by the Gospel to men of our time, but she believed no less that the Gospel is the Word of God, not one word of God among others, but *his* Word in a fullness that is unique.

When we have returned to that point, or simply reached it, we can start out again, but not before.

But for that, as for the rest, we must not be content with pious wishes. We must see clearly the realistic means that will give us back a living and missionary Church, and we must have the courage to return to it. This is perhaps what is most difficult.

The reforms the Church needs more urgently than ever are to be found for the most part in the three areas of the clergy in general, the laity and the episcopate. But they are all dominated by a basic problem which is one of culture.

Catholic Christianity, i.e. true and integral Christianity, is no more one culture than it is one political action, even taking this last word in its most exalted sense which has, unfortunately, not much in common with what we call politics today. But if it is true that we cannot conceive of a Christianity which would not become translated into action on a civic level, it is even harder to conceive of it developing otherwise than in a culture. Let us repeat once again that Christianity is a truth of life, and culture is nothing else than the thought that informs the whole of human life, or that life becoming conscious of itself, by all the means of meditation and reflection at man's disposal. A Christianity which does not think about itself, or which would want to think of itself as outside of life, of all of life, is not feasible. Properly Christian thought is not only the affair of specialists to whom it could be left as their own particular concern. It is and must be of interest to all Christians to the extent of their capacities. But it is first of all of interest to the clergy who have the task of forming and maintaining the life of their brother. St. Francis de Sales said plainly that in his youth, the word "priest" had become synonymous with "ignorant" and "profligate." We are not yet at that point, but we are getting there fast. The clergy is losing the sense of the requirements of asceticism, and even of morality, in their vocation. Some time ago—half a century at least—it had begun to lose the sense of its intellectual requirements. As a result of the repression of modernism those responsible for its formation were persuaded that the less the clergy knew, the "safer" would be its training. Did we not see a few years before the Council the appearance of an episcopal document that asserted that since heresies were the doing of theologians, they had to be held closely in check, and limited (*under the lash*, as Newman said) to explaining to others only the statements authority would produce without their cooperation? Far from improving since the Council, the situation has abruptly worsened. A great many seminaries are now merely schools for batting the breeze, where everything is talked about, but nothing is seriously studied, and above all no one learns how to study.

The task of the theological faculties has never been solely to form seminary professors but to maintain among the clergy an intellectual elite which is as necessary for the life of the parishes and the different movements of the apostolate as it is for the formation of clerics in general. The present concern of the episcopate, in France at least, seems to be to replace them in this latter task by super-practical institutes in which the teachers of future clergy-men would be trained only in what is called catechesis and pastoral theology (which in the concrete signifies, three quarters of the time today, a pedagogy without doctrinal content and the esoteric word games in which too great a part of Catholic Action has become entangled). As for their other task, the faculties have long been unable to fulfill it, because the bishops seem to have forgotten for years that a good theological formation is desirable not only for future professors, but for all the priests called to im-portant pastoral responsibilities. The idea, admitted by the Germans, that *all priests*, today especially, need a univer-sity-level theological formation, in France still seems, and more than ever, to be a pure scandal. As long as we fail to do this, the future of the whole Church will remain stymied. If there is one point in France on which the Church seems to be in accord with the Republic is that she too is con-vinced that it has no need of scholars. We should never have arrived at the mess we are in if we were not in the same difficulty on this point. But far from any of this changing, everything done and projected at present tends only to aggravate the situation.

There would be too much to say about this, and I prefer for the moment to stop here. This has been quite enough for people to cry "shame!" at me.

Since Clement and Origen, there is no need to demon-

strate the fact that theological culture cannot grow outside
of the general cultural climate. Particularly, if we want
tradition to remain alive by unceasingly readapting itself
to the needs of the times, this is a condition *sine qua non.*
However, there is the rub: people want to be open to the
world, in fact that is all they talk about, but they do not
want to pay the price. To become intelligently informed
about the progress in research in all the humane sciences,
philosophy, philology, history, psychology, ethnology, the
history of comparative religions, is the primary task. And
reflection upon the physical and biological sciences, on all
the problems raised by the development of technology is
not of lesser importance. And when we are instructed in
these investigations, and trained to pursue them, a Christian reflection becomes necessary; it is one of the primary
tasks of the Christian philosophers, aided by the theologians.

Who among us is seriously interested in that? An un-
critical reading of a few pages of Teilhard de Chardin seems
largely sufficient for most professional Catholic intellectuals. Rhapsodies on technological progress, the Marxist
dialectic or a paper-back psychoanalysis seem the maximum
we can expect of the clergy destined to work with laymen
who have something to do with these problems.

However, a properly Christian culture, and its capacity
to open itself to human culture in general, does not rely
solely on scholarly research, however important that may
be. It presupposes a substructure, or rather a fertile soil,
into which everyone, the most cultivated Christians as well
as the most ignorant, must plant their roots; it is itself the
basic ground for this culture. This substructure, this soil,
can be constituted for us only by the liturgical life in all
is human and sacral fullness, with the living interpretation

of the Word of God that it alone can procure for us.

Once again, at this point, we must speak plainly: there is practically no liturgy worthy of the name today in the Catholic Church. Yesterday's liturgy was hardly more than an embalmed cadaver. What people call liturgy today is little more than this same cadaver decomposed.

Once again there would be too much to say on this subject. Perhaps in no other area is there a greater distance (and even formal opposition) between what the Council worked out and what we actually have. Under the pretext of "adapting" the liturgy, people have simply forgotten that it is and can only be the traditional expression of the Christian mystery in all its spring-like fullness. I have perhaps spent the greater part of my priestly life in attempting to explain it. But I now have the impression, and I am not alone, that those who took it upon themselves to apply(?) the Council's directives on this point have turned their backs deliberately on what Beauduin, Casel and Pius Parsch had set out to do, and to which I had tried vainly to add some small contribution of my own. I do not wish to vouch for the truth, or seem to, at any greater length, of this denial and imposture. If any are still interested, they may read the books I wrote on the subject; there are only too many of these! Or better, they might read the works of the experts I have just mentioned, on whom they have been able to turn their backs, even though the Council approved the essential points of their works, and added nothing of particular value to them. When one has thrown everything out, people will have to return to these sources. As for me, while waiting, I shall concern myself with other tasks which are more in my line: in any case, for me, "the night is coming, where no one can work any more." I have done enough in this area, but to no avail if we can judge by the present results. I prefer not to be obstinate, and I shall go on to something else.

All of the foregoing bears directly on the training of clerics, and of the laity as a rebound. But I am very far from believing that when that is said, one has said everything. Nothing seems more urgent to me today than to have priests trained directly for their ministry by solid studies and a piety nourished at the source. But again, for this they must first be men, and men of their times (not openmouthed nincompoops, bleating at every novelty, but men matured by the experience of life).

In this regard, to ordain twenty-five year old boys, who rush forward to be called "Father!" (remember Knock: "Call me Doctor!") by men who could have been their fathers, is a nameless absurdity. No ordination to major orders ought now to be conferred on men less than thirty, and no one ought to be admitted into a seminary without having completed higher studies and worked in the field towards which these studies were directed for at least a year, or without having received an equally complete manual training, whether as a worker or a farmer, and earned his bread and butter for some time in this way. I am very much afraid that as long as we do not do this, we shall merely have eunuchs in the priesthood, or (what is no better) grown-up adolescents who are incapable of ever escaping a state of hebephrenia.

It is useless to add that men who have gone through these experiences would not tolerate even for a week the life in our contemporary seminaries, with all its empty chatter without content and its "experiences" without object!

Now to the laity. I shall not treat the problem of Catholic Action here. But that its present evolution poses a

problem is to say too little. No one has yet dared to speak
of it openly, because, as one of the most esteemed French
bishops told me recently: "Catholic Action is scarcely more
today than one of Potemkin's churches, a cardboard
church, maintained by the future bishops for the intellectual
and spiritual comfort of the present bishops." I limit myself to quoting literally, without comment, since I am not
one of their group. But one does not have to be one of their
number to realize that Catholic Action, after having propagated the sound practice of "revision of life," if it is not
capable of following it rigorously itself as quickly as possible, will either die a natural death, or else kill the Church
it was supposed to regenerate.

While waiting, no one can ignore another problem. The
great majority of the best Catholic laymen, rightly or
wrongly, will not hear of joining these "movements," such
as they have become. What are we waiting for before we
become aware of such a glaring fact?

At a time when we are speaking of allowing the laity to
speak, shall we continue to let only a handful of them speak,
and ignore the existence of the others?

And finally, the episcopate! A few months ago I was dis-
cussing the present situation in the Church with an African
bishop who is not only one of the best bishops from the
black continent, but one of the best in the contemporary
Church. With that beautiful beguiling smile with which God
has brightened the darkest faces of mankind, he told me:
"What do you want! The Church after the Council is somewhat in the same situation as our African armies. We have
made generals overnight out of people chosen and trained
to be nothing more than master-sergeants. Nothing will
ever be able to work while we still have this situation." I
admit that it seemed to me that that bishop put his finger

right on *the* present-day sore afflicting the episcopate.

Rome is paying today for her faults of yesterday, but we too have to pay with her, and it is for the bishops themselves that the bill is most burdensome.

Politics dictated by fear is regularly the most harmful, and in regard to the nominations of bishops, since the first Vatican Council, Rome seems to have been dominated by the possibility of a return to Gallicanism. Consequently, wherever she could, she turned down from the episcopate not only thinking men, but even men of character, beginning with the pastors who seemed to have suceeded too well in the priesthood of second rank. Good administrators moved as little as possible by initiatives, or chaplains of Catholic Action (which down to our day is still considered above all, in Italy, as a nursery for the "Volunteers of the Pope," ecclesiastical analogues, minus the tone, of the supporters of the royalist party) : these and these alone could be episcopable. Fortunately, nuncios are not omniscient, and it has happened more than once that they let pass through their nets, little fish who they never dreamed could grow big, such as Emmanuel Suhard and a few others, to speak only of the dead. And then there remained in Germany or Switzerland, a few vestiges at least of the traditional election . . . and even places where the governments retained a power of presentation, which did not always have such bad effects, and finally a few others like the United States where a nomination by co-optation became practically the *de facto* rule (this ran the risk of maintaining friendly cliques, but not always).

It is very fine to speak of episcopal collegiality,, but for it to become a reality, we should first have to refashion a doctrine of the episcopate (that would discover something other than mitered pen-pushers or chaplains general of

Catholic Action, which is what the present situation has become), and then to choose men who are not only nice chaps (they all are!) but men who are qualified to be, in reality and not only in principle, pastors, doctors, and priests. It says very little that we have not yet reached this point! The doctrine has to be completely rethought, and especially rediscovered. Nominations that would conform to it, ought to be made in a manner that is obviously quite different from what it is at present. But, it is not a democratic-type election that will make matters right. All this would do at present would be to intensify the combat of the blind in the Church, between integralists and progressivists. A balanced *modus vivendi* of consultations among the chapters (which must become again *real* chapters and not merely asylums for harmless old men), the representatives of the clergy of all grades, representatives of *all* the laity, and finally of the Holy See (as is done in Switzerland) would probably be the best we could wish for today, as the results seem to show.

For the moment, all these things are merely beautiful dreams with which to entertain ourselves. As yet they do not have the slightest beginning of being realized, and on every point, one could buoyantly embark on quite different courses. Let us hope that one day out of an excess of tribulation, the necessary reaction will take place, which, without daring a prediction, we should like to think was not far off. If I am not mistaken, and with me the numberless priests, more numberless bishops than one might believe, and many others in the Church who have been thinking and saying quietly for a long time what I have just tried to say out loud, it will be necessary to direct ourselves along paths that may not be exactly what I have just outlined, but which have a good chance of resembling them quite closely.

While waiting, the experience of the ministry, of the fraternity of work and concerns among so many generous, industrious and clear-sighted priests which the Church still possesses (even though they are hardly ever consulted and people in high places are especially busy keeping them in step and in making them regularly pay their tribute) and then so many of the faithful, whose patience, faith, and charity are a constant comfort to those who know them differently than through trumped up sociological surveys, will help those who believe in the Church founded upon the Rock, and of which Christ is the cornerstone, to persevere in the assurance that his Spirit has not abandoned it, and that it will bounce back, purer and more radiant, from the unnameable abyss into which it has been plunged today.

And if the "real Catholics," whether of the Right or the Left, stubbornly keep it down, the Orthodox and many Anglicans and Protestants who have not ceased to love it or who have relearned to desire the one true Church will help us to draw it out of the abyss despite our "real Catholics."

As for what is called "Catholicism," a word which appeared only, if I am not mistaken, in the 17th century (if by this we understand the artificial system fabricated by the Counter-Reformation, and hardened by the cudgeling of modernism) it can die. There are even good chances that it is already dead, even though we do not perceive it. The one, holy, catholic and apostolic Church, over which Peter and his successors "preside in charity," has the promise of eternal life, and its faith shall not be deluded.